D1305675

PRACTICE
MAKES
PERFECT

Spanish Pronouns
Up Close

Eric Vogt, Ph.D.

Mc
Graw
Hill

New York Chicago San Francisco Lisbon London Madrid Mexico City
Milan New Delhi San Juan Seoul Singapore Sydney Toronto

1 2 3 4 5 6 7 8 9 10 11 12 13 14 15 16 17 18 19 20 21   FGR/FGR   0 9 8

ISBN 978-0-07-149224-9
MHID   0-07-149224-0
Library of Congress Control Number: 2006937322

Interior design by Village Typographers, Inc.

McGraw-Hill books are available at special quantity discounts to use as premiums and sales promotions or for use in corporate training programs. To contact a representative, please visit the Contact Us pages at www.mhprofessional.com.

This book is printed on acid-free paper.

Contents

Acknowledgments

My earnest thanks go to Garret Lemoi at McGraw-Hill for his patience as I prepared the final version of this book—and for so enthusiastically urging me to write it in the first place. Likewise to Susan Moore for her diligence and sharp eye.

As ever, I thank Lylje Klein for noticing every point that needed clarifying. I also thank my students who, during the 2007–2008 year, used earlier versions of these chapters and commented on their usefulness.

No amount of thanks will ever be enough to tell my family how much I've missed them while they've waited for me on Bainbridge Island as I've worked late nights in Seattle on this and other projects over the past two years.

Introduction

Keeping track of pronouns in Spanish can be a bit frustrating for learners who do not know the names and jobs of these various players on the linguistic playing field as well as the rules of the grammar game that determine what job they perform. But take heart. Pronouns, one of the parts of speech along with articles, verbs, nouns, adjectives, and so on, consist of a small number of little words with big jobs to do. They tell you *who* is doing something or *who* is giving *what* to *whom*, together with a host of other functions that we examine in this book.

Pronouns are words that stand in for a noun. Nouns, you may recall, are names of people, places, things, or feelings (John, Susan, Chicago, table, bird, flower, love, anger, . . .). *He* (**él**) is used instead of *John*, if John is the subject and the speaker and listener already have mentioned John by name. If John is the object, *him* (**lo**) stands in for *John*. Although it is not always the case, in both English and Spanish the form of a pronoun often indicates its grammatical function:

Él (Juan) corrió en la lluvia al partido.
Yo **lo** (Juan) vi resbalarse en el hielo.

He (John) ran to the game in the rain.
*I saw **him** (John) slip on the ice.*

Let's indulge in a grammatical analogy using baseball to introduce you to the communicative richness of this small group of words known as pronouns. First, we will learn the names of three of the main types of pronouns and discover what their roles are on the language-learning playing field. (Of course, if the influences in your life happen to be British, you might have to make some quick mental adjustments to adapt the names of the positions on the field to cricket, but we *Yanks* trust that you will follow along just fine.)

When a person is doing something, he or she is the actor—the active agent of an action. The action itself is expressed by a verb. In baseball, the most common actions are batting, catching, and throwing. When a batter steps up to the plate, bat in hand, awaiting the pitch, he awaits an action on the part of the pitcher on the mound.

From a grammatical point of view, at the opening of the game the pitcher is the *subject* when he throws the ball, because he is the one *who* throws it. The ball is *what* he throws; thus, grammatically speaking, the ball is the *direct object*. A direct object receives the action of a verb directly. In our analogy, the action, expressed by the verb, is the pitch.

While the ball is hurling through the air at 90 miles per hour or more, the batter is waiting to become the next subject—that is, the one who will hit the ball (or, if you happen to be a Chicago Cubs fan, the one who will *strike* at it—and miss, of course). For a split second—the moment the ball makes contact with the bat—the batter can be seen grammatically as the *indirect object*, the *one who receives* the direct object of the ball. However, the instant he swings the bat and hits (or strikes), he is the doer, or grammatical subject. In fact, he is the subject on the field at that moment. Everyone else is awaiting the result, as anxious fans will confirm. If he strikes, the catcher, in like manner, is the indirect object at the moment the ball contacts his glove, at which instant he becomes the subject of the verb *to catch*, and then, remaining the subject, he performs another action, throwing the ball back to the pitcher.

Each of the three players—pitcher, batter, and catcher—has been either subject or indirect object in his own way during the quick action from first pitch, to hit or strike, to catch, and to throw the ball again. The names of those positions in fact denote the role of that player as doer (subject) of a particular action (verb). In our analogy, the ball, of course, never does anything on its own; it never is the subject. It has been only a direct object. However, the ball *is* the subject if one says, "The ball flew out of the park" or "The ball rolled between the outfielder's feet."

In the following four examples, all the pronouns, **yo, ella,** and **ellos** (*I, she, they*) are *subject pronouns*. They represent the person or people doing something. It is important to observe that in Spanish, there is no subject pronoun to correspond with the English pronoun *it*.

Yo tiré la pelota.	*I threw the ball.*
Ella va a la tienda.	*She goes to the store.*
Ellos dieron una fiesta.	*They gave a party.*
Es un día bello.	*It is a beautiful day.*

In the following four sentences, all the pronouns, **lo, nos,** and **la** (*him, us, it*) represent someone or something understood, often previously stated or alluded to in context (both examples of **la** refer to an object that is feminine in gender—**la pelota** and **la carta**). Note particularly how these pronouns receive the action of the verb directly (such as a physical blow or even a glance). Since they represent people or things that are acted upon directly, they are known as *direct object pronouns*:

El boxeador **lo** tumbó.	*The boxer knocked **him** down.*
Teresa **nos** ve.	*Teresa sees **us**.*
El jugador **la** tiró.	*The player threw **it**.*
Mamá **la** escribió.	*Mother wrote **it**.*

In the examples that follow, the pronouns **le, les,** and **me** (*him, them, me*) represent receivers of something, concrete (such as a gift) or abstract (such as permission). They are *indirect object pronouns*:

Juan **le** da un reloj.	*John gives **him** a watch.*
La maestra **les** dio permiso para salir.	*The teacher gave **them** permission to go outside.*
Mamá **me** escribió una carta.	*Mother wrote **me** a letter.*

From the previous examples it should be clear that in order to comprehend what you read or hear, or to say what you mean to say, you have to have a clear mental picture of the three concepts of *subject*, *direct object*, and *indirect object*. Most, if not all, people do this unconsciously in their native language. But it is not enough to grasp the concepts or abstractions. You also need to know the forms that correspond, sometimes uniquely, to each of these functions. Sometimes, of course, one form, such as *him*, *you*, or *it* can fulfill a number of roles. Thus, context is very important. The same is true of the forms in Spanish.

Fortunately, there are not a great number of pronoun forms, fewer than two dozen in fact. The baseball analogy is helpful only insofar as it may enable you to grasp the concepts. This book is designed to help you proceed to learn the forms that are used for those grammatical functions and to understand and use them correctly. More will be said about subject, direct object, and indirect object pronouns in their respective sections and, while it is true that there are more types of pronouns than these three, the baseball analogy helps get you started. The other functions presented and examined in this book will come more easily once these three basic concepts are understood.

Be sure to read all the sections in the order in which they appear, and be sure to do all the exercises after you have read and are reasonably sure that you understand each chapter. In order to simplify the exercises and allow you to concentrate on the task of learning all the Spanish pronouns and their proper uses, the verbs usually appear in the present indicative tense. Almost certainly you have bought this book because you have had problems with pronouns, so it is almost as certain that your difficulty in one area may be the result of an imperfect understanding of another. The order in which the pronouns are presented conforms with the order in which they most frequently are presented in textbooks, but they are examined in greater detail, with quizzes and answer keys along the way.

What makes pronouns challenging is the ironic fact that they are few in number but have deceptively similar-looking forms and several of them even have multiple uses, as you have seen. Without doubt, the most troubling of these are the four functions of **se**. But all in good time.

Subject pronouns

Subject pronouns indicate who is the doer (or doers) of an action, but there is another, intimately related purpose to knowing the subject pronouns and what they mean: in Spanish, the conjugation of verbs is far more important than it is in English. In the present tense, for instance, English distinguishes only the third person singular from all the other persons and numbers (*I, we, you, they* **go**, but *he, she,* or *it* **goes**). In the other tenses and moods, English does not vary the forms of verbs. By contrast, Spanish varies the verb form for nearly every person and number, although in some tenses and moods the first and third person singular forms are identical. This makes it all the more important to have a perfect knowledge of the subject pronoun forms and the verb endings that correspond to them in each and every tense and mood. There will be some practice in the exercises of this chapter to reinforce the relationship between pronouns and their corresponding verb endings (in the present tense only), after doing some exercises to reinforce the conceptual aspect of person, number, and their associated forms.

One of the more common problems students have when confronted with the concept of subject pronouns is that they often confuse the concept of what the *grammatical subject* of a sentence is with the rhetorical question of what the *topic* of a sentence is. When you hear or read *Tom is a committed pacifist*, the grammatical subject of the sentence is *Tom*, whereas the topic may or may not be Tom. More context, often a paragraph, would be necessary to determine whether Tom, or perhaps pacifism, is the topic. One lesson here is that it is relatively easy to identify a subject (*Tom*) and verb (*is*), because you need only identify who is doing something, or about whom or what something is being said. In the following examples, **niños** (*boys*) is the subject of **construyeron** (*built*) and **lluvia** (*rain*) is the subject of **duró** (*lasted*):

Los **niños construyeron** un
    castillo de arena.
La **lluvia duró** todo el día.

*The **boys built** a sandcastle.*

*The **rain lasted** all day.*

Another lesson to be learned from these sentences is not to overthink the problem when identifying the grammatical subject of a sentence. As you examine the examples and work through the exercises, don't go beyond what a sentence allows you to conclude. In a nutshell, don't invent context.

Once the concept of grammatical subject is clear, the next hurdle for English-speaking students of Spanish is to realize that each subject pronoun has a corresponding verb ending in every tense. There is often psychological resistance to this way of thinking. A need to hold on to what is familiar may at times prevent you from being willing to be open to adventure. To embark on learning a foreign language requires leaps of faith to clear the hurdles along the way.

In English, each verb has five forms only—for example: *sing, sings, sang, sung,* and *singing.* The first two forms belong to the present tense, in which the final *s* is a sign of the third person singular (i.e., *he, she,* or *it*).

In Spanish, there are fourteen tenses, each with three persons, singular and plural. Doing the math reveals what at first seems a daunting reality—that there are eighty-four forms for every verb, plus two participles and the infinitive. When one recalculates that number by discounting the instances in which the first and third persons singular share one form, it can still be an intimidating number. And beginners through advanced students struggle with the task of sifting through irregular verbs.

Without a doubt, for students of Spanish, verbs stand alone as a special area of study. Yet many of the difficulties encountered in the study of verbs are easily solved by first gaining a clear understanding of the forms of the subject pronouns and their respective meanings, which correspond to their assigned verb endings. As soon as most students properly align the other pronoun forms, their functions, and meanings (e.g., indirect and direct objects) with the same matrix as the subject pronouns, many problems of comprehension and oral proficiency begin to melt away. The matrix uniquely identifies all pronouns in terms of the person and number to which they refer.

Grammatically, there are *three persons* in Spanish and *two numbers* (singular and plural). By definition, the *first person* refers to oneself alone (in the singular) or to oneself with others included (in the plural), in all their various grammatical functions. The first person singular is comprised of the subject form **yo** (*I*), and one additional form that functions as the first-person singular's indirect, direct, and reflexive pronoun, **me** (*me*). The first person plural is comprised of **nosotros** and **nosotras** (*we*) and **nos** (*us*) for almost all the object functions. The subject pronoun **nosotras** is reserved for females only. Absolutely no hint of sexism can be attributed to the fact that Spanish employs the masculine inclusive in its pronoun system, nor does the grammatical or lexical notion of gender inclusiveness, all too prevalent in English-speaking societies, have any meaning in Spanish.

The *second person,* grammatically, is the person or people to whom one is speaking—in other words, whatever is meant by the English pronoun *you.* In standard Spanish there are four ways to say *you* (a fifth form, **vos**, used in a region of Latin America is discussed later in this chapter). It is easy enough for English speakers to accept that there are two forms corresponding to *you* even though English does not vary the form for the singular and plural, familiar and formal meanings of this second person pronoun.

Let's take a closer look at each of the four forms that translate into English as *you*. But before we proceed, remember that the *second person* is defined as the person or people to whom one is speaking, which logically includes all forms of *you*. This observation applies even to the formal terms, **usted** and **ustedes**, which employ the *third person* verb forms, for reasons that will be explained when we examine these pronouns.

The subject pronoun **tú** is the second person singular form, used when addressing a person one considers an intimate friend or social equal. This applies of course to the form *te*, which is used for almost all the instances in which a second person singular familiar person is in any way the object of a verb. Thus, Spanish retains a dimension that English lost when *thou* and *thee* ceased to be used.

The plural form of **tú** is **vosotros** (and, when addressing an exclusively female group of friends, **vosotras**). The **vosotros** form is used almost exclusively in Spain. It is encountered elsewhere in scripture, sometimes in liturgical use, and in literature, movies, and other artistic productions of peninsular origin—that is, the Spanish spoken in Spain. It is almost never encountered in natural speech in Latin America. In fact, many, if not most Spanish-speaking people in the rest of the world do not know how to form the verb forms associated with this pronoun, and so it is often omitted or glossed over in Spanish-language instruction outside Spain. This situation is analogous to the teaching of American or British English: the dialect taught depends on the dialect of the teacher, the program, the country in which English is taught, and so forth. At any rate, the proper use of the **vosotros** form with its corresponding verb forms is easily acquired if one has a strong command of the verb system and already is adept at using the familiar **tú** and the formal **usted** forms.

Of all the subject pronouns, the second person singular, **usted**, and its corresponding plural form, **ustedes**, are the most interesting from a historical perspective. For students of Spanish, the concept of grammatical person is often lost and errors result from a lack of attention as to why (and how) it came about that while these two subject pronouns are *second person in meaning*, they still require the use of their respective third person verb forms, and also share the object pronoun forms used by the other, truly third person pronouns. Much attention then, must be paid to the third person throughout the pronominal system.

The form **usted** is derived from **vuestra merced** (literally, *your mercy*, analogous to the English expression, *your grace*). Likewise, the plural, **ustedes**, is derived from **vuestras mercedes**. Both these forms of address were ways to avoid the familiar **tú** when speaking to strangers or people of superior rank. In fact, unlike other European languages, Spanish did not have a single-word formal form of address for the subject pronoun *you* until relatively recently. The modern forms **usted** and **ustedes** (often abbreviated as **Ud.** and **Uds.**, respectively) began to stabilize around the end of the seventeenth century due to constant repetition of the original expressions.

What has not changed is that each of these pronouns, although *second person in meaning*, have retained their strict correlation with the *third person* verb forms. It is essential to keep this in mind because not only the verb forms but also the other pronouns corresponding to the third person (**se**, **le**, **les**, **lo**, **la**, **los**, and **las**) are used in relation to the **usted** and **ustedes** forms. These other forms—various types of object pronouns—will be examined in their respective chapters.

Grammatically speaking, the *third person* is the person or people about whom one or more people are speaking. The third person pronouns are **él** and **ella** (*he* and *she*, singular) and **ellos** and **ellas** (*they*, masculine and feminine plural). Because **usted** and **ustedes** are second person in meaning, but take third person verb forms and share the third person object pronoun forms, it is the third person forms, especially the objective forms, that are most troublesome to learners. Each form will be dealt with in turn. For now, it is enough to understand the forms and uses of the subject pronouns in Spanish:

	SINGULAR	PLURAL
FIRST PERSON	yo	nosotros, -as
SECOND PERSON	tú	vosotros, -as
THIRD PERSON	él	ellos
	ella	ellas
	usted	ustedes

Finally, no discussion of Spanish subject pronouns would be complete without an explanation of the subject pronoun **vos**. While this form is heard in certain regions of Latin America, such as in the densely populated Venezuelan coastal city of Maracaibo, it is most commonly used in Argentina and other nearby countries, in the region known as Rioplatense or Cono del Sur.

During the period of intense colonization in the sixteenth and seventeenth centuries, **tú** was the pronoun of choice for addressing inferiors or equals for whom one felt the strongest degree of familiarity. When addressing others, even those for whom some degree of intimacy was felt, **vos** was used. During this same period, **vuestra merced** was beginning to be used generally as a means of formal address, which reinforced the use of **tú** for intimate address. But not all regions adopted this innovation equally, and in fact, there are some anomalies, such as the Andes region of Venezuela or among some portions of the population in Bogotá, where **usted** is used among friends and even family members. Almost all the Spanish-speaking Americas eventually adopted **ustedes** as the only plural form (corresponding to the plural use of *you* in English).

The verb endings used with **vos** are derived from the **vosotros** forms, but with some modification (as a rule of thumb, the *i* is dropped from the ending, but the stress on the last syllable is retained). The best advice to nonnatives is to learn the standard Spanish well, before venturing into the deep end of the dialect pool.

Finally, the best types of exercises for gaining a command of the subject pronouns require learners to bear in mind that subject pronouns stand in for nouns. Often these nouns are people's proper names. The exercises that follow are designed to increase learners' mental agility in switching points of view. This is an essential skill when asking and answering questions and otherwise engaging in the give-and-take of conversation. Since verbs must agree with their subjects in person and number, and since the verb forms are so distinct, it is important to remember that the ability to manage the shifting perspectives of subject pronouns in a conversational exchange ultimately must be directed at managing the proper alternation of their corresponding verb conjugations. This is easily illustrated with the following everyday exhange. Note as well that the verb form used also changes in agreement with the change in grammatical subject.

¿Cómo estás **tú?**	*How are **you**?*
Yo estoy bien.	*I am fine.*

The challenge for learners of Spanish is that they must become conscious of what they do instinctively in their own language. While it is intellectually obvious, there is a great gulf between appreciating the abstraction and being able to apply it quickly. If you have ever listened to children learning to talk, you will recall how they have difficulty with this. To cite one example, small children use their own names to refer to themselves before they realize that when they hear the word *I*, it stands for whoever is speaking about him or herself. This is one of the earlier stages of language development that takes some time to master. The advantage you, the postadolescent learner, has is that you can grasp the abstraction. But you still need the practice.

EJERCICIO
1·1

Give the English subject pronoun that corresponds to each of the following Spanish subject pronouns or people indicated.

1. ella _____

2. Juana _____

3. él _____

4. mi papá _____

5. Julio y yo _____

6. yo _____

7. ustedes _____

8. Juan y María _____

9. nosotros _____

10. tú _____

11. vosotros _____

12. tú y tus hermanas _____

13. vosotras _____

14. usted _____

15. el Sr. González _____

Give the Spanish subject pronoun equivalents of the following brief phrases—that is, give the pronoun that would be used when the following are subjects of a sentence. Note: When you see you, *remember that the exercise is talking to* you, *the student. Think of yourself speaking from the page. For example, if you see:* you (my brother), *the answer would be* **tú**, *because that is the pronoun you would use to address him (with the corresponding verb ending when forming a complete sentence).*

1. he _____

2. you (*my aunt*) _____

3. my sister and I _____

4. I _____

5. you and Sr. González (*not your intimate friends*) _____

6. you (*my classmates*) _____

7. María and Teresa _____

8. Juan and Tomás _____

9. Tomás and María _____

10. you and Juan (*friends of yours*) _____

11. we _____

12. you (*my boss*) _____

13. you (*Teresa and Juana* [*friends of yours*]) _____

14. you (*Sr. Gómez and Sr. Suárez*) _____

15. my coworkers and I _____

16. they (*all males*) _____

17. the boys _____

18. the male boss _____

19. the boss and his wife _____

20. she _____

21. you (*my uncle*) _____

22. his uncle _____

23. you (*my friend*) _____

24. her friend Juan _____

25. my friend María _____

In the following exercise, give the Spanish pronoun that would be the subject of an answer directed to, or about, the person or people indicated.

EXAMPLES   ¿Quién? ¿Tú? ___Sí, yo.___

¿Quiénes? ¿Tomás y Roberto? ___Sí, ellos.___

1. ¿Quién? ¿Juan? _____

2. ¿Quién? ¿Yo? (*between strangers*) _____

3. ¿Quiénes? ¿María y Teresa? _____

4. ¿Quién? ¿Yo? (*between friends*) _____

5. ¿Quiénes? ¿Los señores Gómez? _____

6. ¿Quién? ¿Aquella señorita? _____

7. ¿Quién? ¿Ese médico? _____

8. ¿Quiénes? ¿Los miembros del club? _____

9. ¿Quién? ¿El amigo de Enrique? _____

10. ¿Quiénes? ¿Esos estudiantes? _____

11. ¿Quién? ¿Mi hermana? _____

12. ¿Quiénes? ¿Los primos de Marta? _____

13. ¿Quién? ¿El presidente? _____

14. ¿Quiénes? ¿Mis hermanos? _____

15. ¿Quién? ¿Tu papá? _____

16. ¿Quién? ¿Esa maestra? _____

17. ¿Quiénes? ¿Aquellas niñas? _____

18. ¿Quién? ¿Este chico? _____

19. ¿Quiénes? ¿Juan y yo? _____

20. ¿Quiénes? ¿Tú y tu hermano? _____

Make identical statements about other subjects using the subject pronouns given. Recast the sentence using the proper conjugation in the present indicative tense of the conjugated verb found in the original sentence. No other changes are necessary.

1. Juan habla español. Tú...

_____

2. Ellos ven la película. Yo...

_____

3. Mi amiga corre mucho. Ellos...

_____

4. Yo tengo una hermana. Él...

_____

5. Su padre va a Honduras. Mi amigo...

_____

6. Tú y yo leemos el periódico. Ellas...

_____

7. Mis padres trabajan en la ciudad. La mamá de Enrique...

_____

8. Juanita viaja a España este verano. Yo...

_____

9. Yo como el desayuno en la cafetería. Usted...

_____

10. Los Gómez viven en Guadalajara. Ustedes...

_____

11. Mi padre paga con tarjetas de crédito. Yo...

_____

12. Ellos prefieren jugar en el jardín. Mi hija...

_____

13. Él necesita estudiar más. Mi hermana y Juana...

_____

14. Tú compras comida en el mercado. Nosotros...

_____

15. Ellas escriben cartas todos los días. Vosotros...

_____

16. El Sr. Valdez vende motocicletas. Ellos...

_____

17. Nosotros le damos flores a nuestra mamá. Mi papá...

_____

18. Su mamá nos visita los fines de semana. Tú...

_____

19. Ellas piensan mucho en las películas. Su hermano...

_____

20. Yo duermo ocho horas cada noche. Mis hijos...

_____

EJERCICIO
1·5

Form simple questions using the subject pronouns and verbs given. Use the present indicative tense only.

EXAMPLE   tú/comprar   _¿Tú compras?_

1. ella/mirar _____

2. él/ir _____

3. yo/estudiar _____

4. Enrique y María/viajar _____

5. ellas/ver _____

6. nosotros/dormir _____

7. tú/leer _____

8. tú y yo/escribir _____

9. nosotros/necesitar _____

10. Juan/buscar _____

11. ellos/poner _____

12. usted/volver _____

13. yo/tener _____

14. yo/estar _____

15. ustedes/decir _____

16. tú/salir _____

17. la Sra. Martínez/pagar _____

18. mis tíos/salir _____

19. yo/ser _____

20. vosotros/trabajar _____

Fill in the blanks with the correct form of the main verb from the opening question. The verb should agree with the grammatical subject (subject pronoun) of the second sentence. Use the present indicative tense only.

1. ¿Compra Juan en el mercado? Sí, y yo también _____ en el mercado.

2. ¿Va Luisa al cine mucho? No, y su hermana tampoco _____ al cine mucho.

3. ¿Puedo ir al parque solo, mamá? ¿Solo? No, tú no _____ ir al parque solo.

4. Juana, ¿me acompañas al teatro? ¡Cómo no! Claro que yo te _____ al teatro.

5. ¿Se ponen los zapatos los niños? Sí, ahora los niños se _____ los zapatos.

6. ¿Voy a la playa ahora o no? ¡Claro! Espérate. Nosotros _____ a la playa también.

7. ¿Cambias la camisa por los pantalones? Sí, yo la _____ por los pantalones.

8. ¿Tus amigos escuchan música clásica? No, ellos _____ rock.

9. En el restaurante, ¿qué pides? Yo _____ camarones o pollo asado.

10. ¿Trabaja tu novio en el centro? Pues, los dos—él y yo— _____ en el centro.

11. ¿Quién sirve la comida en el restaurante? Los meseros _____ la comida.

12. ¿Qué debo pedir de postre? Tú _____ pedir el platillo de fruta fresca.

13. ¿A qué hora sales para el trabajo, Juan? Yo _____ a las siete de la mañana.

14. ¿Qué piensan ustedes de la situación económica? Nosotros _____ que está grave.

15. ¿Siempre cantas en las fiestas? Yo no, pero mi novia sí; ella siempre

_____ .

16. ¿Vuelven tus amigos después de ver la película? No, ellos no _____ entonces.

17. ¿Vas a llevar esa falda esta noche, María? No, ésa la _____ a llevar tú.

18. ¿Pones flores en la mesa? Sí, yo las _____ en la mesa.

19. ¿Cuánto sabes tú de la física atómica? ¿Yo, de la física atómica?

No _____ nada.

20. Yo siempre sigo los deportes, ¿y tú? Yo no, pero mi hermano los

_____ .

Reflexive object pronouns

The first reflexive verb students of Spanish are exposed to in introductory chapters of most textbooks is often unaccompanied by any grammatical analysis, explanation, or warnings. You may recall seeing the question **¿Cómo te llamas?** and its corresponding answer **Me llamo** _____ in a preliminary chapter to your text. These use, of course, conjugated forms of the verb **llamarse**. It is important to realize that the verb **llamar** is not reflexive. The verb **llamar** simply means *to call*. Adding the third person reflexive pronoun to the infinitive creates a reflexive infinitive, **llamarse**, which means *to call **oneself***. This verb is introduced early in most Spanish programs in the hope that students will absorb the concept of reflexivity and also avoid literal translation from the English statement *My name is* _____, resulting in **Mi nombre es** _____, which is less commonly used in Spanish conversation than **llamarse**. However, as we are about to explore, there are ways to categorize and thus predict how other verbs can be or become reflexive.

Verbs that have to do with personal hygiene are usually reflexive. For instance, **bañarse** means *to take a bath* when it is not reflexive (*bañar*), but it will mean that someone (the subject) is bathing someone else.

Baño al bebé.	*I bathe the baby.*

To say **baño** alone, or even **yo baño** communicates only *I bathe* without any indication of who is being bathed. Therefore, in the following English translations, "oneself" or "one's" is used to indicate that the action is to be understood as reflexive. In Spanish, the reflexivity is communicated simply by appending **se** to the infinitive, creating the reflexive infinitive, as we saw when we reviewed the difference between **llamar** and **llamarse**.

bañarse	*to take a bath*
cortarse las uñas	*to cut one's nails*
cepillarse los dientes	*to brush one's teeth*
ducharse	*to take a shower*
lavarse las manos	*to wash one's hands*

peinarse el cabello	*to comb one's hair*
ponerse los pantalones	*to put on one's pants*
vestirse	*to dress oneself, get dressed*

With verbs related to hygiene or other matters of personal care, such as dressing one-self, the use of the reflexive verb eliminates the need for a possessive adjective (as in *I'm washing **my** hands*). As the next examples show, the possessive is necessary—or at least is often used in English—to show whose hands are being washed or whose shirt a person is putting on. Reflexive pronouns do not denote possession. Definite articles are used instead of possessive adjectives, but definite articles, used without the context of the reflexive pronoun, do not denote possession.

Hence, reflexive pronouns simply make a possessive adjective needless at best, redundant at worst. Of course, if there were a specific reason to introduce more information, possessive adjectives could be used. But normally, it is assumed, thanks to the reflexive pronoun, that the hands being washed are those of the subject, or that the shirt the person is putting on belongs to the person putting it on.

Los niños se lavan **las** manos.	*The children wash **their** hands.*
Él se pone **la** camisa.	*He puts on **his** shirt.*

Many verbs that indicate emotional states and health also are often expressed with reflexive object pronouns. When not used reflexively, object pronouns indicate that the grammatical subject and the receiver are not the same person or people. In the following examples, consider the differences between the verb **enojar**, which means *to anger*, and its reflexive form **enojarse**, which means *to become angry*:

Juan **me** enoja.	*John angers me.*
Me enojo con Juan.	*I get angry with John.*

The first example makes Juan the subject and the cause of the speaker's anger. Juan is the one doing the angering and the speaker is the direct object, as shown by the fact that the verb agrees with Juan (the third person subject, equivalent to **él**) and also by the use of **me**, an object pronoun. In the second example, even though Juan somehow may be responsible for the speaker's anger, the speaker is not directly pointing the finger of blame. The speaker is merely observing that, for whatever reason, he or she becomes angry with Juan. Another way to look at the use of the reflexive in the second example is to conceptualize the anger as something that arises from within the speaker, not from some outside cause, which may, in fact, be the case, if Juan is not to blame at all. The anger comes from within the subject, him or her*self*. It is easy to see that the speaker is the subject by the use of the first person singular form of the verb, **enojo**, even though the subject pronoun **yo** is not used. Because of this, the use of **me** can only be interpreted as reflexive. Thus the speaker is subject and reflexive object at the same time.

In order to translate these reflexive infinitives into English, and thus understand what the reflexive form is doing in Spanish, either *become* or *get* are used indiscriminately when translating the following and similar examples. Sometimes a preposition or some modifier is used in English following the verb, a structure known as a phrasal verb. Many phrasal verbs in English are rendered as reflexives in Spanish, such as the examples **caerse** and **levantarse** below.

aburrirse	*to get bored*
alegrarse	*to become happy*
caerse	*to fall down*
cansarse	*to get tired*
dormirse	*to fall asleep*
enfermarse	*to get sick*
enojarse	*to become angry*
entristecerse	*to become sad*
levantarse	*to get up*

Now that we have revisited what you have likely been exposed to in your language study up to this point and revealed some logical categories of reflexive verbs, we arrive at a practical definition of what *reflexivity* is all about. When someone performs an action and is also the receiver of the action, a reflexive object pronoun is used that shows that the action reflects back on the doer.

When one considers that personal hygiene often involves using a mirror, the image of reflexivity becomes very easy to conceptualize and remember with confidence. In the following example, observe that, in Spanish, the subject pronoun is **yo**, the verb is conjugated to agree with the subject in person and number (first person singular), and the reflexive object is **me**. Note, too, that it is placed immediately before the conjugated verb. The positioning of subject-object-verb is a typical structural feature of Spanish sentences, but not the only one. It may take some getting used to, but it is essential to become accustomed to this word order so as to not become lost. Until the next chapter, which deals with direct object pronouns, we will only show the positioning of the object pronoun before the conjugated verb of a sentence, as in the following examples. Note how this subject-object-verb order is applied in both affirmative and negative sentences:

Yo **me** veo en el espejo.	*I see **myself** in the mirror.*
Yo no **me** veo en el espejo.	*I do not see **myself** in the mirror.*

Expanding on these examples, let's look at all the possible reflexive objects, according to person and number, beginning with the singular forms:

Yo **me** veo en el espejo.	*I see **myself** in the mirror.*
Tú no **te** ves en el espejo.	*You do not see **yourself** in the mirror.*

Él **se** ve en el espejo.	*He sees **himself** in the mirror.*
Ella no **se** ve en el espejo.	*She does not see **herself** in the mirror.*
Usted **se** ve en el espejo.	*You see **yourself** in the mirror.*

In comparing these sentences with each other and with their English translations, a number of valuable observations can be made that will help you keep subjects and objects straight. First, subject pronouns have forms that are distinct from each other and from their corresponding reflexive object forms. The subject pronoun **yo** has, for instance, the corresponding reflexive object **me**. Second, note that the verbs are conjugated to agree with the subject pronouns (**él/ve**). The third observation is really a reminder. The **usted** form is second person in meaning but shares the verb forms and object forms of the third person. In fact, the reflexive object corresponding to both singular and plural third person subjects is **se**. Now, examine the plural forms:

Nosotros **nos** vemos en el espejo.	*We see **ourselves** in the mirror.*
Vosotros **os** veis en el espejo.	*You see **yourselves** in the mirror.*
Ellos no **se** ven en el espejo.	*They do not see **themselves** in the mirror.*
Ellas **se** ven en el espejo.	*They see **themselves** in the mirror.*
Ustedes **se** ven en el espejo.	*You see **yourselves** in the mirror.*

There is an additional interpretation possible for the plural forms only that can be determined only from context. It is possible to see many reflexive actions as mutually reflexive. That is, we may see *each other* in the mirror, or they may see *each other* in the mirror, and so forth. Using the verb **besar** (to kiss) it is easy to see how the very meaning of this verb makes anything but a mutually reflexive interpretation absurdly comical:

Ellos **se** besan.	*They are kissing (**each other**, not themselves).*

Examining the forms reveals there are only five to learn—five tiny little one-syllable words, and one of them (**os**) used only in Spain! There is potentially more good news. As will be seen in greater detail and with more explanation in the following chapters, the forms **me**, **te**, **nos**, and **os** are also the forms used for direct and indirect objects, context being the means by which they are interpreted. In fact, there are only six more forms to learn in order to complete the picture of reflexive, direct, and indirect objects. The most important word of advice is to keep close track of the forms and meanings of the third person forms, since that is where the greatest source of confusion is found. To summarize, the reflexive object pronouns are:

	SINGULAR	PLURAL
FIRST PERSON	me	nos
SECOND PERSON	te	os
THIRD PERSON	se	se

In addition to verbs of hygiene, health, and emotion, there are other verbs that are, or can be, reflexive. The reflexive is often used to emphasize an action or to lend a sense of urgency. At first, some learners are a bit perplexed to see a verb become reflexive when there seems to be no real reason for it. Verbs of motion, for example, can become reflexive in form, but there is no appreciable difference in meaning between the reflexive and the nonreflexive uses. Consider the following examples, noting how the Spanish reflexive examples have to be rendered into more colloquial English to capture the emphatic tone:

Juan **se** va de aquí.	*John is getting out of here.*
Juan va.	*John is going.*
Me voy.	*I'm heading out.*
Voy...	*I'm going . . .*
Nos vamos.	*We're out of here.*
Vamos...	*We're going . . .*
¿**Te** vas?	*Are you taking off?*

As you proceed to the exercises, keep in mind that the five object pronouns we have learned (**me, nos, te, os,** and **se**) comprise a very small but powerful set of markers. When used with verbs conjugated to agree in person and number with the person and number of these pronoun forms, they are known as reflexive object pronouns. The identical reference with regard to person and number among subject, verb, and object confirms and indicates that the action performed by the subject reflects back on the doer or doers.

EJERCICIO
2·1

Conjugate the following reflexive verbs in the present indicative tense, according to the subject pronouns indicated. Then translate your example into English.

EXAMPLE   enojarse/él   *Él se enoja. He gets mad.*

1. levantarse/yo

_____

2. acostarse/ella

_____

3. ponerse/yo

_____

4. dormirse/vosotros

_____

5. cansarse/él

_____

6. verse/ella

_____

7. despertarse/nosotros

_____

8. enfadarse/yo

_____

9. secarse/tú

_____

10. preocuparse/tú

_____

11. entristecerse/usted

_____

12. maquillarse/ellas

_____

13. alegrarse/ustedes

_____

14. deprimirse/ellos

_____

15. lavarse/nosotros

_____

16. reírse/yo

_____

17. enfermarse/él

_____

18. ducharse/ustedes

_____

19. mojarse/ellas

_____

20. cepillarse/vosotros

_____

Select the sentence that uses the correct reflexive construction to translate the sentences given in English. Note that all the options are grammatically correct sentences.

1. The children fall down.
   a. Los niños me caen bien.
   b. Los niños se caen.
   c. Los niños lo dejan caer.

2. His mother gets sick.
   a. Su madre está enferma.
   b. Su madre es enferma.
   c. Su madre se enferma.

3. We get tired.
   a. Estamos cansados.
   b. Somos tediosos.
   c. Nos cansamos.

4. They become sad.
    a. Ellos se entristecen.
    b. Ellos me entristecen.
    c. Ellos están tristes.

5. My friends laugh.
    a. Mis amigos cuentan chistes.
    b. Mis amigos se ríen.
    c. Mis amigos están alegres.

6. My wife puts on makeup.
    a. Mi esposa usa maquillaje.
    b. Mi esposa se maquilla.
    c. Mi esposa se compra maquillaje.

7. They hug each other.
    a. Ellos lo abrazan.
    b. Ellos me abrazan.
    c. Ellos se abrazan.

8. I am worried.
    a. Me preocupo.
    b. Me preocupa.
    c. Estoy preocupado.

9. The players put on their shoes.
    a. Los jugadores llevan zapatos.
    b. Los jugadores se ponen los zapatos.
    c. Les ponen los zapatos a los jugadores.

10. They go to bed before the children.
    a. Los niños se acuestan antes que ellos.
    b. Ellos se acuestan antes que los niños.
    c. Ellos acuestan a los niños.

11. He falls asleep quickly.
    a. Él duerme mucho.
    b. Él está dormido.
    c. Él se duerme rápidamente.

12. They get happy.
    a. Ellos son felices.
    b. Ellos se alegran.
    c. Ellos están contentos.

13. We get sick.
    a. Nos enfermamos.
    b. Somos enfermos.
    c. Estamos enfermos.

14. I get depressed.
    a. Estoy deprimido.
    b. Me deprimo.
    c. Me deprime.

15. We get up early.
    a. Estamos despiertos temprano.
    b. Nos levantamos temprano.
    c. Nos levantan temprano.

16. They get dressed.
    a. Ellos llevan ropa.
    b. Ellos se visten.
    c. Ellos están vestidos.

17. He gets bored.
    a. Él se aburre.
    b. Él está aburrido.
    c. Él es aburrido.

18. They kiss each other.
    a. Les gusta besar.
    b. Ellos se besan.
    c. Ellos besan.

19. We look at each other.
    a. Nos miramos.
    b. Nosotros miramos.
    c. Estamos mirando.

20. She gets angry with John.
    a. Ella se enoja con Juan.
    b. Ella está enojada con Juan.
    c. Juan la enoja.

Translate the following simple English sentences into Spanish.

1. John falls asleep.

   _____

2. Theresa and Mary wake up.

   _____

3. You and I get up.

   _____

4. My friends fall down.

   _____

5. You (*formal, singular*) get angry.

   _____

6. The children hug each other.

   _____

7. My mother gets happy.

   _____

8. Thomas and Joe get sick.

   _____

9. Her friends laugh.

   _____

10. He and I are worried.

    _____

11. We get tired.

    _____

12. She gets depressed.

    _____

13. Thomas and Joe get better.

   _____

14. They put on makeup.

   _____

15. I get sick.

   _____

16. She becomes sad.

   _____

17. She and I kiss.

   _____

18. They see each other.

   _____

19. They take a shower.

   _____

20. We wash our hands.

   _____

Direct object pronouns

In this category, you will need to learn only four new words in addition to **me**, **te**, **nos**, and **os**. As pointed out in the previous chapter, these four pronouns vary their function according to their relationship with the subjects and verbs they are used with. We have seen them only as reflexive objects, but now they will be examined along with the four new pronouns (**lo**, **la**, **los**, **las**) that function specifically as direct objects of verbs.

To identify the direct object, one uses the verb in the sentence to ask the question *what* or *whom*. Thus, in order to identify the direct object noun in the following sentences, you need only to ask the following questions: *What* does John cut? *Whom* does John see? *What* does John see?

Juan corta **la manzana**.	*John cuts **the apple**.*
Juan ve **a Marcos**.	*John sees **Mark**.*
Juan ve **el perro**.	*John sees **the dog**.*

The answers to these questions are obviously *the apple*, *Mark*, and *the dog*. When a speaker and listener have already stated these nouns in a conversation, object pronouns are used in their place in order to avoid monotonous repetition. There is an additional feature to be learned in the second sentence—the use of the preposition **a** to mark a noun as an object or, if you prefer, to mark it as a nonsubject. Since word order is much more flexible in Spanish than in English, if this little word (known in this grammatical circumstance as the *personal* **a**) were left out, especially when the subject and object are both third person (*and* either singular or plural), it would be impossible to tell who does the action (the subject) from who receives the action (the object). The *personal* **a** is used only when a human being is an object of a verb, as shown by the third sentence: John sees the dog (although when the dog, or other animal, is a beloved pet, the *personal* **a** is often used, which shows just how much people tend to humanize their pets). This feature will become more important in the next chapter on indirect objects, and even more important when a verb has two objects.

As for the choice of direct object pronoun, in Spanish **la manzana** is feminine and singular, and so the feminine third person direct object pronoun **la** is used. Likewise, **lo** replaces both Marcos and the dog (assuming the dog is male).

Juan **la** corta.	*John cuts **it**.*
Juan **lo** ve.	*John sees **him**.*
Juan **lo** ve.	*John sees **him*** (or at least a singular masculine *it*).

Because Spanish is a language that depends heavily on grammatical gender, two forms are needed to express the English word *it*: **lo** and **la**. **Lo** and **la** are also used for *him* and *her*, respectively, as well as for *you* (formal, singular), when the pronoun *you* is not the grammatical subject. For the corresponding plural forms in the third person, **los** and **las** mean *them* (people or things) or *you*, again, as the plural direct object, when the pronoun *you* (formal, singular) is not the grammatical subject. To summarize, these are the direct object pronouns:

	SINGULAR	PLURAL
FIRST PERSON	me	nos
SECOND PERSON	te	os
THIRD PERSON	lo	los
	la	las

One common error among English speakers is to attempt to use **lo** as a subject pronoun. In Spanish, there simply is no subject pronoun that corresponds to the way *it* is used as a subject in English. It is true that **lo**, along with **ello**, **eso**, **esto**, and **aquello**, are neuter pronouns that can be objects or subjects, but these are not exact equivalents of *it* even when they may seem to be so. (**Ello** and **aquello** are generally not used in conversation, but rather in writing.) Neuter pronouns are used to refer to something that cannot be assigned a gender, such as a vague topic or general reference that cannot easily be reduced to a single noun:

Lo de ayer fue interesante.	*What happened yesterday was interesting.*
Eso puede ser.	*That could be.*
Esto es algo que no entiendo.	*This is something I do not understand.*

The neuter pronoun **lo** is also commonly encountered in answers to questions in which it substantivizes some abstract quality, such as friendship in the following exchange:

—¿Eres mi amigo?	*"Are you my friend?"*
—Sí, **lo** soy.	*"That I am."*

Because of the high probability of confusing these neuter pronouns with the English uses of *it* as a subject pronoun, it might be wise for intermediate- and even advanced-level speakers to avoid attempting to use them as subject pronouns and to become used to simply omitting the subject pronoun when the English translation would place *it* at the beginning of a sentence, as these very common expressions exemplify:

Llueve.	**It** *is raining.*
Es interesante.	**It** *is interesting.*
Es un buen plan.	**It** *is a good plan.*

Even though **lo** cannot be used *on its own* as a subject pronoun equivalent to the pronoun *it* in English, the use of **lo** plus an adjective creates an abstract subject whose usage is very common and therefore necessary to learn and use with confidence. Consider the following examples and it will be easy and obvious how you can invent others in like manner, simply by following **lo** with an adjective (the word *thing* may also be substituted by *part*). Often, these types of expressions are found at the beginning of sentences, to introduce anecdotes from daily life. They can be further intensified by using **más** or **menos**, as some of the following examples show:

lo bueno	*the good thing* (or *the good part*)
lo terrible	*the terrible thing*
lo más interesante	*the most interesting thing*
lo bello	*the beautiful thing*
lo más increíble	*the most incredible thing*
lo menos agradable	*the least agreeable part*

There are two main reasons why managing direct object pronouns in Spanish is a bit challenging for English speakers. It may seem odd why this mere handful of words should present so many challenges. Big things come in small packages, and these little words are powerful markers. They have to be handled with care—that is, they must be used with great precision with regard to the gender and number of the noun they represent and also with regard to position.

The first challenge, gender and number agreement, is problematic for English speakers because English nouns, except for those that refer to animals and people, generally have no grammatical gender. A table is a table to an English speaker and is neither masculine nor feminine (in reality or grammatically). Of course, English speakers have no problem with using *he* or *she* (subjects) or *him* or *her* (objects) when speaking of a bull or a cow, a rooster or a hen, and John or Mary. What English speakers need to do is to realize, and accept, that in Spanish, these biologically based gender distinctions expand, in a manner of speaking, to include all nouns. This non–biologically based gender is, from a practical point of view, quite arbitrary and, in common parlance, is called *grammatical gender*.

Let's first examine the problems posed by gender and number. In Spanish, **una mesa** is *feminine* and *singular*. On the other hand, even though **los pantalones** (*trousers*) refers to one article of clothing, it is, as in English, *plural* and *masculine*. The fact that nouns have gender and number imposes a requirement on speakers to ensure that when a noun is the subject of a verb, the verb and subject agree with regard to person and number. If a conversation is about a table, then **la** would be understood by the speakers to refer to the table, until and unless some other feminine singular direct object noun is named. Likewise, **los** would refer to pants in a conversation which both speakers know is about pants.

Thus, when a noun is turned into a pronoun, it has to agree with that noun in gender and number. The challenge for learners is to keep track of the gender and number of the noun being replaced. The ease or difficulty in doing this depends on the richness of one's vocabulary and the precision with which one has learned it. One of the principal solutions to the vocabulary challenge and, by transference, to the task of keeping track of the gender and number of direct object pronouns, is to learn vocabulary by preceding each noun by the correct definite article (**el**, **la**, **los**, or **las**). It is to the learner's great advantage to recognize the value of this method, since all the definite articles are identical in form to the direct object pronouns, with the exception of the masculine singular, **lo**.

—¿Viste al maestro?	*"Did you see the teacher?"*
—Sí, **lo** vi.	*"Yes, I saw **him**."*
—¿Limpiaste los zapatos?	*"Did you clean the shoes?"*
—Sí, **los** limpié.	*"Yes, I cleaned **them**."*
—¿Dónde está la maleta?	*"Where is the suitcase?"*
—**La** tengo aquí.	*"I have **it** here."*
—¿Quién compró las flores?	*"Who bought the flowers?"*
—Juan **las** compró.	*"John bought **them**."*

Whether through travel, in print or movies, or with a new professor, sooner or later every student of Spanish will discover that there are two distinct camps in the Spanish language, defined by whether the speaker uses **lo** or **le** as the masculine singular direct object pronoun. These two camps are known as **loístas** and **leístas**, respectively. On numerous occasions, the Royal Academy of the Spanish Language has stated clearly its preference for the **loísta** camp. To shorten the Academy's argument, use **lo** when referring to the *masculine singular direct object*, not **le**. Still, do not be surprised should you encounter instances of **le** being used in the same situation. In fact, all the direct object pronouns, singular and plural, are confused by some speakers and used as indirect object pronouns. Sometimes whole regions are infected with this grammatical error. Nevertheless, the Academy begrudgingly considers **le** to be an admissible alternative to the (proper) use of **lo**, and even then, the Academy admonishes writers and teachers to try to enforce limiting the use of **le** to that of an indirect object pronoun. In the next chapter, this category of pronouns is examined and explained in detail.

The other challenge English speakers face when dealing with object pronouns concerns the rules for the proper placement or position of direct object pronouns. Learners should take heart though, because there is only one brief set of rules covering the allowable placement of all object pronouns, not just the direct object pronouns. As promised in the previous chapter, it is now time to examine all the possible positions in which object pronouns of any kind may be placed, using only the direct object pronouns we have just examined.

Placing the object pronouns before the conjugated verb is one of the most reliable rules because it is the one that is permissible in all cases, except where affirmative commands are concerned (when they must follow the verb and be attached to it). Placing object pronouns before the conjugated verb was the position in which we placed the reflexive object pronouns in the last chapter. Applying this rule to direct object pronouns, examine the following examples:

Ella **me** saluda.	*She greets **me**.*
Nosotros **lo** vemos.	*We see **it/him** (or you—formal, singular).*
Tú no **la** escribes.	*You do not write **it** (with this verb, **la** is inanimate).*
Usted **nos** envía a Europa.	*You send **us** to Europe.*

When there is only one conjugated verb, there is no other placement option for object pronouns. When an auxiliary verb (also known as a helping verb) is used, followed by a complementary infinitive, then one other possibility arises. The object pronoun may be attached to the infinitive, as in the following examples:

Yo quiero escribir**la** ahora.	*I want to write **it** now.*
Ella no espera ver**me** mañana.	*She doesn't expect to see **me** tomorrow.*
Nosotros necesitamos mandar**los**.	*We need to send **them**.*
Tú tienes que mencionar**lo** en la reunión.	*You have to mention **it** in the meeting.*

Keep in mind that you still have the option of placing the object pronoun before the conjugated verb. What is absolutely not allowed is to place the object pronoun between the auxiliary verb and the complementary infinitive (or indeed between any type of helping verb and any form it can introduce, as we will see in a moment). The above sentences could just as well be spoken or written as follows, with absolutely no change in meaning:

Yo **la** quiero escribir ahora.	*I want to write **it** now.*
Ella no **me** espera ver mañana.	*She doesn't expect to see **me** tomorrow.*
Nosotros **los** necesitamos mandar.	*We need to send **them**.*
Tú **lo** tienes que mencionar en la reunión.	*You have to mention **it** in the meeting.*

The next common situation is when using the progressive, which is formed by any conjugation of the verb **estar** (in any tense) followed by the gerund (corresponding to the *-ing* form in English). When this happens, an accent must be placed on the originally accented syllable of the gerund, since otherwise the accent would shift to the new next-to-the-last syllable, thus mangling the pronunciation. The accent was not needed when the syllable was appended to the infinitive, because infinitives are all automatically stressed on their infinitive ending.

The possible placements for the object pronouns in this case are exactly the same as when using a helping verb and a complementary infinitive: either following and attached to the gerund, or before the conjugated form of **estar**. Once again, the object pronoun can *never* go between them:

Ella está mir**á**ndo**las**.	*She is looking at **them**.*
Nosotros estamos escrib**ié**ndo**la**.	*We are writing **it**.*
Él no está prepar**á**ndo**los**.	*He is not preparing **them**.*
Yo no estoy plant**á**ndo**las**.	*I am not planting **them**.*

As before, the object pronoun also can precede the conjugated verb, with no change in meaning:

Ella **las** está mirando.	*She is looking at **them**.*
Nosotros **la** estamos escribiendo.	*We are writing **it**.*
Él no **los** está preparando.	*He is not preparing **them**.*
Yo no **las** estoy plantando.	*I am not planting **them**.*

When dealing with command forms, there are no options for placement, no matter if the command be formal or familiar, singular or plural. For affirmative commands, the pronoun (or pronouns, as future chapters will show) *must follow and be attached to* the command. For negative commands, they *must immediately precede the command*. The following examples should suffice to make this rule very clear, even if you still have some difficulty with the formation of the commands themselves:

¡Mánda**las**!	*Send **them**!*
¡No **las** mandes!	*Don't send **them**!*
¡D**e**lo!	*Give **it**!*
¡No **lo** dé!	*Don't give **it**!*
¡Cré**ame**!	*Believe **me**!*
¡No **lo** crea!	*Don't believe **it**!*

Match the following nouns and subject pronouns with the direct object pronoun that would replace them. It is possible that each may be used either more than once or not at all.

1. _____ mi papá		a.	las
2. _____ mi mamá		b.	nos
3. _____ tú		c.	lo
4. _____ yo		d.	te
5. _____ tú y yo		e.	me
6. _____ Juan y Teresa		f.	la
7. _____ el teléfono		g.	los
8. _____ Juana y María		h.	os
9. _____ mis gatos			
10. _____ la mesa			

For each of the following nouns or subject pronouns, give the corresponding direct object pronoun that would replace them. Of course, you may need—and use—a dictionary.

1. yo _____

2. la hamburguesa _____

3. yo y mis amigos _____

4. the houses _____

5. a computer _____

6. the fork _____

7. tú _____

8. the cake _____

9. a pencil _____

10. an automobile _____

11. three shirts _____

12. vosotros _____

13. the information _____

14. my dog _____

15. Tomás y Roberto _____

16. you (*formal, singular*) _____

17. nosotros _____

18. their parents _____

19. nosotras _____

20. él _____

EJERCICIO
3·3

For each of the following very short sentences, indicate whether direct object pronouns should be placed before the verb (B), *or whether they could be placed either* before the verb *or attached to a verbal complement (E). By highlighting the verb or verb phrase, these rather skeletal sentences serve to reinforce the possibilities for placing object pronouns.*

1. _____ Juan ve.

2. _____ Tú estás escribiendo.

3. _____ Ella compra.

4. _____ Teresa desea exportar.

5. _____ Nosotros vamos a pedir.

6. _____ Mis padres envían.

7. _____ Sus amigos esperan abrir.

8. _____ Yo evalúo.

9. _____ Susana odia.

10. _____ Usted va a servir.

11. _____ Juana y Carlos necesitan producir.

12. _____ Tú debes borrar.

13. _____ Yo alquilo.

14. _____ Mis padres ven.

15. _____ Tú puedes usar.

16. _____ Los científicos determinan.

17. _____ El cartógrafo mide.

18. _____ El carpintero va a cortar.

19. _____ Los músicos quieren tocar.

20. _____ Nosotros podemos aumentar.

EJERCICIO
3·4

This exercise contains four steps: a. Translate each of the following sentences, using the direct object noun. b. Identify the direct object noun in each. c. Determine the proper direct object pronoun that should replace each direct object noun. d. Rewrite the sentences, replacing each direct object noun with the proper direct object pronoun. For those sentences that contain helping verbs-plus-infinitive or the progressive, write two sentences in order to demonstrate the two optional positions in which the direct object pronoun can appear in Spanish.

EXAMPLE   He wants to buy cookies.

    a.   *Él quiere comprar galletas.*

    b.   *galletas*

    c.   *las*

    d.   *Él las quiere comprar./Él quiere comprarlas.*

1. We bring the food.

   a. _____

   b. _____

   c. _____

   d. _____

2. She sees María.

   a. _____

   b. _____

   c. _____

   d. _____

3. They should tell the story.

   a. _____

   b. _____

   c. _____

   d. _____

4. You (*familiar, singular*) read the books.

   a. _____

   b. _____

   c. _____

   d. _____

5. He writes a letter.

   a. _____

   b. _____

   c. _____

   d. _____

6. You (*formal, plural*) send the gifts.

    a. _____

    b. _____

    c. _____

    d. _____

7. She is going to buy a coat.

    a. _____

    b. _____

    c. _____

    d. _____

8. They want to sell the house.

    a. _____

    b. _____

    c. _____

    d. _____

9. We make the bread.

    a. _____

    b. _____

    c. _____

    d. _____

10. You (*formal, singular*) rent an apartment.

    a. _____

    b. _____

    c. _____

    d. _____

11. They reduce pollution.

    a. _____

    b. _____

    c. _____

    d. _____

12. He directs the orchestra.

    a. _____

    b. _____

    c. _____

    d. _____

13. She loves her children.

    a. _____

    b. _____

    c. _____

    d. _____

14. They prepare the meals.

    a. _____

    b. _____

    c. _____

    d. _____

15. He is going to leave the sweets on the table.

    a. _____

    b. _____

    c. _____

    d. _____

16. We are going to count the shirts.

    a. _____

    b. _____

    c. _____

    d. _____

17. He is putting the book on the table.

    a. _____

    b. _____

    c. _____

    d. _____

18. I use wine to cook.

    a. _____

    b. _____

    c. _____

    d. _____

19. She can solve the problem.

    a. _____

    b. _____

    c. _____

    d. _____

20. I need to cover the motorcycle because it is going to rain.

    a. _____

    b. _____

    c. _____

    d. _____

Form commands, using the elements given. Change the direct object nouns with the most succinct pronouns and position them according to the rules. Omit the subject pronoun in your answer (this is shown simply to indicate which form of the command you need to use). Watch the gender of the nouns; the articles have been omitted, so it will be a good review of this important feature of the language, one that has to become automatic.

1. tú/no vender/auto

_____

2. tú/traer/botellas

_____

3. nosotros/no romper/vasos

_____

4. Ud./limpiar/ventanas

_____

5. tú/mirar/a Juan

_____

6. tú/no mirar/chicas

_____

7. Ud./escribir/carta

_____

8. Uds./mandar/paquetes

_____

9. Ud./vestir/niños

_____

10. Ud./no poner/pies en la mesa

_____

11. Ud./no distribuir/panfletos

_____

12. Ud./arreglar/cama

_____

13. tú/ayudar/a nosotros

_____

14. tú/quitar/pies del sofá

_____

15. tú/no gritar/a mí

_____

16. Uds./sacar/muebles

_____

17. nosotros/vender/casa

_____

18. tú/abrir/cortinas

_____

19. tú/no tocar/estufa caliente

_____

20. Ud./borrar/error

_____

Translate the following commands according to the people indicated, changing the direct object nouns to pronouns. This will probably require you to review the command forms as well as vocabulary. Take heart: It has to be done if you are to master the language. If you are rusty, the most important aspect of this exercise is to identify the direct object pronoun needed in Spanish and determine its position with relation to the verb in the imperative form.

1. Wash the dog! (**tú**)

   _____

2. Throw the ball! (**Ud.**)

   _____

3. Don't yell at us! (**Uds.**)

   _____

4. Let's prepare dinner! (**nosotros**)

   _____

5. Look at the photo! (**tú**)

   _____

6. Burn the leaves! (**Uds.**)

   _____

7. Don't open the door! (**tú**)

   _____

8. Bring the clothes! (**Ud.**)

   _____

9. Drive the car! (**Uds.**)

   _____

10. Let's not make the chicken! (**nosotros**)

   _____

11. Look for the cat! (**tú**)

_____

12. Clean your room! (**tú**)

_____

13. Don't forget the plates! (**Ud.**)

_____

14. Pay the bills! (**tú**)

_____

15. Don't wear that skirt! (**tú**)

_____

16. Wear this sweater! (**Ud.**)

_____

17. Tell the truth! (**tú**)

_____

18. Don't tell a lie! (**tú**)

_____

19. Read the book! (**Uds.**)

_____

20. Don't rent the apartment! (**Ud.**)

_____

Indirect object pronouns

This chapter adds only two words, **le** and **les**, which are the third person singular and plural forms, respectively, of the indirect object pronouns. Although there are regional differences in the usage of the various forms of the object pronouns that learners will almost certainly encounter as they socialize or read items from around the Spanish-speaking world—and that will run counter to the usage in this book!—the rules presented here are those of the Spanish Royal Academy. It is wise to follow their prescriptive approach to usage: if you do, you can be sure you will be understood wherever you go in the Spanish-speaking world.

Learners will find that they face only one small curveball as they learn the forms and master this category of pronoun usage. As always, the object pronouns **me**, **te**, **nos**, and **os** vary their function according to their relationship with the subjects and verbs they are used with. Having seen how they can be used as reflexive *and* direct object pronouns, we will be examining them, as well as the two new forms, **le** and **les**, in their role as marking the *indirect object* of a verb.

Just as we asked the question *what* or *whom* to identify the direct object of an action, we again have a question that will enable us to identify the indirect object of a verb. Again, the main verb or verb phrase of the sentence is used to form the question, but to find the indirect object, one asks *to whom* or *for whom* the action is performed. In order to identify the indirect object *noun* in the following sentence, you need only to ask the question "*to whom* does John give the apple?" The word order does not change the answer to the question in the two formulations of the example below:

Juan **le** da la manzana **a María**.   *John gives the apple **to Mary**.*
Juan **le** da **a María** la manzana.   *John gives **Mary** the apple.*

In the previous chapter the *personal* **a** was used to mark a human being (or beloved pet) as a direct object. Although the same preposition is used in the examples above, here it introduces a prepositional phrase to clarify to whom the indirect object pronoun is referring. While clarifiers are not necessary if both speaker and listener are "on the same page," the indirect object pronouns must always be used if there is an indirect object (a receiver) involved. In other words, the sentences would not be grammatically correct in Spanish had **le** been omitted.

Such clarification is especially important with the third person indirect object pronouns **le** and **les**, which can refer to three distinct people. The singular, **le**, can be clarified by **a él**, **a ella**, or **a Ud**. Likewise the plural, **les**, can be clarified by **a ellos**, **a ellas**, or **a Uds**. Of course, instead of **a él**, for instance, one could say **a Juan** to clarify **le**; instead of **a ellas** to clarify **les**, one could say **a Teresa y María**, and so forth. It is interesting, and sometimes helpful to learners, to notice that in English, when Mary is moved to the end of the sentence, it also requires the preposition *to* in order to mark her as the indirect object. She is not the doer of the action, but the receiver of the thing (the apple) that directly receives the action that John performs, the *giving*.

To return to our baseball analogy, it is as if the ball were in play in a rapid sequence of *swing*, *hit*, and *catch*. John would represent the batter, the ball would represent the apple, and Mary would represent anyone in the outfield to whom the ball flies (of course, in the instant that the ball is caught, the person catching it is simultaneously the indirect object of the verb *to hit*, but note that he or she is the subject of a *new* action—*to catch*—not the old action, *to hit*). Each word is marked or inflected in some way to show its position on the grammatical playing field. John and the verb *to give* agree in person and number. Mary is marked as an indirect object by the preposition **a**, and the apple logically is the only thing that can be the direct object of the verb.

There is a morphological difference between direct and indirect object pronouns, which manifests itself only by comparing their respective third person forms. Unlike the third person direct object pronouns, the third person indirect object pronouns **le** and **les** do not show gender, but number only.

There is one other small hurdle to jump. When dealing with two object pronouns, the indirect always precedes the direct, according to the same position rules presented in the last chapter. This commonly results in having a third person indirect object pronoun, **le** or **les**, in a situation where it would be followed by the third person direct object pronoun **lo**, **la**, **los**, or **las**. When this happens, **le** and **les** must be changed to **se** to avoid the unpleasant sound of the two short words beginning with the letter *l-* next to each other. In summary, then, these are the indirect object pronouns in Spanish:

	SINGULAR	PLURAL
FIRST PERSON	me	nos
SECOND PERSON	te	os
THIRD PERSON	le (*or* se)	les (*or* se)

At this point, it is important to summarize the possible combinations of indirect object pronouns followed by direct object pronouns. In most textbooks, this feature is referred to as *double-object pronouns*. In order to avoid conveying a fuzzy notion about their respective functions, it is more effective to explain, and then show, that the *indirect* object pronoun comes first, and the *direct* object pronoun comes second. As you examine the chart, you may wonder why **me**, **te**, **nos**, and **os** were not included in the direct object pronoun column—after all, they also are used as direct object pronouns. This concern will disappear if you consider that when dealing with verbs that take two objects (known as "ditransitive" verbs), it would seldom make sense if, for instance, **me** were the indirect object and **te** the direct object.

One could, however, imagine some contexts in which some combination of indirect object on the left column might be followed by these same forms—as direct objects, such as in the following sentences:

Me te presentan.	*They introduce **you to me**.*
	(Literally, "To me you they introduce.")
Te me presentan.	*They introduce **me to you**.*
	(Literally, "To you me they introduce.")

The next chart is very useful for figuring out which combinations are by far the most common. It also serves as an easy-to-visualize aid to remind learners what happens when **le** or **les** is followed by **lo**, **la**, **los**, or **las** (they *must* be changed to **se**).

As it turns out, this small collection of one-syllable words, arranged with indirect object pronouns in the left column and direct object pronouns in the right, allows only twenty combinations—which in reality is only sixteen when you recall that **os** is not used typically in the Americas. Observe that any of the indirect object pronouns on the left can *only* be followed by the direct object pronouns on the right, and *only in that order*. That these are the only possible combinations is not the result of any prescriptive grammar rule; it is simply the limited number of possible combinations (i.e., **me lo**, **me la**, **me los**, **me las**, **te lo**, ... , etc.).

INDIRECT	DIRECT
me	lo
te	la
nos	los
os	las
le/les > se	

It is essential to get used to this word order. As you can see immediately, it is quite different from English. **Me lo**, for instance, means either *to* (or *for) me*, followed by the direct object meaning *it, him,* or *you.* For the sake of brevity, in the following examples **lo** is retained as the direct object pronoun. It can only stand in for a masculine singular direct object, animate or inanimate (*it* or *him*). When **lo** means *you,* it stands in as the direct object pronoun for a masculine singular person whom you address formally (i.e., with **Ud.**). If a different direct object pronoun on the list above were chosen, such as **las,** it would stand in for *them* (feminine plural, animate or inanimate). From your study of direct object pronouns in the previous chapter, it should be easy to see how the choice of direct object pronoun will affect the meaning and when you would use one or the other.

Additionally, in these examples the verb **decir** is conjugated for various subjects, but only to remind learners to keep track of *who* the doer of an action is as well as *what* they are doing and *to* or *for whom*—subject, object, and verb forming the most important structural nucleus of a Spanish sentence. Of course, the subject pronoun is usually not stated, since the verb endings convey that semantic information. The examples are meant to focus on what the various indirect object pronouns mean.

Indirect object pronouns standing only for singular "receivers"

Me lo dice.	*He/she* (or *you*—formal, singular) *say/s it to **me**.*
Te lo digo.	*I say it to **you*** (familiar, singular).
Se lo digo.	*I say it to **him/her*** (or *to **you***—formal, singular).

Indirect object pronouns standing only for plural "receivers"

Nos lo dices.	*You* (familiar, singular) *say it to **us**.*
Os lo digo.	*I say it to **you*** (familiar, plural—in Spain).
Se lo decimos.	*We say it to **them*** (or *to **you***—formal, plural).

Whenever two object pronouns are used, they will be placed in that order (indirect *first,* direct *second* and immediately following), regardless of whether they are then placed before a conjugated verb or attached to the end of an infinitive or a gerund. Take a look at the following examples, in which we review the position rules for object pronouns presented in the previous chapter, this time using two object pronouns instead of one. Certain things should be observed in these sentences:

* Whenever the pronouns can be moved to a different position, they move together in relation to the verb phrase, in tandem.
* The alternative placements do not affect the meaning. Remember that if there is only one verb, there is no alternative but to place any and all object pronouns in front of it.

- When pronouns are attached to the end of any of the verb forms they can be attached to, a written accent is placed on the vowel of the syllable that is stressed before adding them. This is done in order to retain the proper stress.
- Command forms (i.e., the imperatives) do not allow any alternative positioning of object pronouns. With affirmative commands, object pronouns are attached; with negative commands, object pronouns are placed between **no** and the verb, and as separate words.
- Finally, when the sentence is negative, the object pronoun or pronouns are sandwiched between **no** and the verb. Note that the subject pronoun **tú** would not be used normally, except for emphasis. It is retained in these examples to reinforce your understanding of the architecture of Spanish sentences. The verb **regalar** means *to give (as) a gift.*

Tú **me las** regalas.	*You give **them to me**.*
Tú no **me las** regalas.	*You do not give **them to me**.*
Tú **me las** quieres regalar.	*You want to give **them to me**.*
Tú quieres regalár**melas**.	*You want to give **them to me**.*
Tú **me las** vas a regalar.	*You are going to give **them to me**.*
Tú vas a regalár**melas**.	*You are going to give **them to me**.*
Tú **me las** estás regalando.	*You are giving **them to me**.*
Tú estás regalándo**melas**.	*You are giving **them to me**.*
¡Regála**melas**!	*Give **them to me**!*
¡No **me las** regales!	*Don't give **them to me**!*

These sentences show all, yes *all*, the possible positions in which object pronouns may be placed in modern, standard, everyday Spanish. Learners should also be delighted to know that these rules apply everywhere in the world, regardless of dialect or any regional idiosyncrasies that might also be present as far as other aspects of the language are concerned, such as pronunciation, vocabulary, or even differences in the choice of pronouns (e.g., **leístas** vs. **loístas**).

Recognizing the proper meaning of the subject-object-verb nexus. Match the Spanish sentences on the left to the English sentences on the right.

1. _____ Me lo dan.

2. _____ Te los da.

3. _____ Se lo dice.

4. _____ Te la contamos.

5. _____ Se la vende.

6. _____ Se las vende.

7. _____ Me la dices.

8. _____ Nos lo envían.

9. _____ Nos las envían.

10. _____ Te los envío.

11. _____ Me los envías.

12. _____ Me las das.

13. _____ Se los regalo.

14. _____ Me los regalas.

15. _____ Te la cuento.

a. *They send us the package.*

b. *I give them the sweaters.*

c. *They give me a hat.*

d. *They send us the lamps.*

e. *I send you the desks.*

f. *You tell me the truth.*

g. *You give me the pencils.*

h. *He gives you the books.*

i. *She says it to them.*

j. *You give me the shirts.*

k. *We tell you the truth.*

l. *I tell you the lie.*

m. *He sells her the house.*

n. *You send me the pants.*

o. *She sells them the magazines.*

Using the elements below, write grammatically correct sentences, changing all object nouns to object pronouns and placing them in the correct position. If there is more than one possible position, write both. Use the present tense only.

1. él/dar/coche/a su hijo

_____

2. ellos/mandar/carta/a mí

_____

3. yo/enviar/paquete/a ti

_____

4. tú/querer entregar/trabajo/a tu jefe

_____

5. ella/ir a regalar/camisa/a su papá

_____

6. nosotros/no querer prestar/dinero/a Enrique

_____

7. yo/no ir a transmitir/mensaje/a mis jefes

_____

8. los jefes/proveer/herramientas/a los trabajadores

_____

9. la compañía/no suministrar/equipo/a Ud.

_____

10. el presidente/ir a conferir/honor/al soldado

_____

11. los vendedores/distribuir/productos/a sus clientes

_____

12. el político/dirigir/discurso/al público

_____

13. yo/no pagar/la cuenta/a ellos

_____

14. ella/no decir/verdad/a mí

_____

15. el maestro/tener que repetir/pregunta/a la clase

_____

16. los niños/escribir/cartas/a los Reyes Magos

_____

17. el reportero/ir a comunicar/noticia/a nosotros

_____

18. el astrónomo/indicar/distancia de las estrellas/a los turistas

_____

19. la asistente de vuelo/decir/la temperatura de la ciudad/a los pasajeros

_____

20. mis padres/dar/permiso/a mi hermana

_____

Form commands, using the elements given, changing the object nouns to pronouns and positioning them according to the rules. (In your answer, omit the subject pronoun, which is only shown to indicate which form of the command you need to use.) Watch the gender of the nouns.

1. Ud./contar/chiste/a los chicos

   _____

2. tú/no contar/chiste/a mis padres

   _____

3. Uds./indicar/respuesta/a los alumnos

   _____

4. vosotros/enseñar/matemáticas/a los niños

   _____

5. tú/dictar/carta/a la secretaria

   _____

6. Ud./mostrar/mapa/a mí

   _____

7. Uds./vender/casas/a los ricos

   _____

8. tú/no decir/mentiras/al jefe

   _____

9. vosotros/entregar/tarea/a la profesora

   _____

10. Ud./conferir/título/a los graduados

    _____

11. tú/enviar/chocolate/a tu esposa

    _____

12. Uds./prestar/dinero/a mi hermano

_____

13. Uds./no prestar/llaves del auto/a los adolescentes

_____

14. Ud./transmitir/información/a nosotros

_____

15. tú/repetir/fórmula/al científico

_____

16. tú/no escribir/mensajes/a mí

_____

17. Ud./no proveer/equipo protector/a los obreros

_____

18. Uds./no dirigir/mirada/a él

_____

19. tú/regalar/diamante/a tu novia

_____

20. vosotros/no pagar/deuda/a ella

_____

Translate the following sentences from Spanish to English. While it is not possible to say what **lo** *and* **la** *(*it*) or* **los** *and* **las** *(*them*) refer to when they have replaced inanimate nouns (such as* **silla**—**la** *or* **escritorios**—**los**)*, you need only translate them here as* it *or* them.

1. Juan me los da.

_____

2. Se lo digo a ellas.

_____

3. Ella me la cuenta siempre.

_____

4. Nos los envía por correo aéreo.

_____

5. Te lo vamos a vender.

_____

6. Van a mandártelos.

_____

7. Se lo estamos leyendo a los niños.

_____

8. Me las vas a comprar.

_____

9. ¡Enséñaselo!

_____

10. Se los voy a distribuir a mis clientes.

_____

11. Ellos nos la van a escribir.

_____

12. Juan se lo repite a los alumnos.

_____

13. Tú se lo indicas en el mapa.

_____

14. ¡No se lo digáis!

_____

15. Yo se lo doy a ellas.

_____

16. ¡Préstemelo!

_____

17. Te la entregan cada semana.

_____

18. Ud. quiere comentárnoslo.

_____

19. Los jefes me lo comunican cada mañana.

_____

20. Él no me lo desea decir.

_____

Translate the following sentences from English to Spanish, replacing all object nouns with the correct object pronouns and placing them in the proper position with regard to the verb or verb phrase. If they can be placed in more than one position, write all versions.

1. We are going to show him the animals.

   _____

2. They want to bring us the gifts.

   _____

3. She is going to send her the magazine.

   _____

4. Do you (**tú**) want to make us a cake?

   _____

5. Buy me a car! (**tú**)

   _____

6. They are not going to dictate the message to us.

   _____

7. I send her flowers.

   _____

8. She tells me the truth.

   _____

9. Are you (**Ud.**) going to lend him money?

   _____

10. She is going to write her mother a letter.

    _____

11. He is buying her a sweater.

    _____

12. The children are distributing the pamphlets.

_____

13. Are you (**Uds.**) going to turn in your work to the teacher today?

_____

14. The teacher does not want to have to repeat the lesson to them.

_____

15. Sell him the horse! (**Ud.**)

_____

16. Repeat the story to me! (**tú**)

_____

17. Tell her a lie! (**Uds.**)

_____

18. They are supplying us the tools.

_____

19. I am going to pay him the money tomorrow.

_____

20. She wants to reveal the data to them tonight.

_____

The uses of se

Now that you have seen the subject pronouns as well as the various forms for the reflexive, direct, and indirect object pronouns, and have done a considerable number of exercises with them, it is important to step back and review the uses of the pronoun **se**. The various functions of this powerhouse pronoun can frustrate learners, so it is essential to focus on this one word and sort out its uses.

In chapter 2, you saw how the pronoun **se** functions as a third-person reflexive object pronoun, both singular and plural. In chapter 4 you saw how it must replace **le** and **les** when these two indirect object pronouns would otherwise be followed by the third person direct object pronouns **lo**, **la**, **los**, or **las**. No mistake about it, the category of third person pronouns is where one encounters different forms for different functions; in this case, the one form, **se**, performs multiple functions, as this quick reminder from previous chapters shows.

These are not the only functions of this pronoun. There are two others, and since they can look deceptively similar to the reflexive use of **se**, we will learn ways to quickly distinguish one from the other as well as use **se** correctly. First, however, let's review the two situations in which we have encountered this interesting object pronoun.

Reflexive **se** compared with **se** in double-pronoun constructions

First, to begin to consolidate the notion of what a reflexive construction really does, consider that reflexive object pronouns are merely a subcategory of indirect object pronouns, in which the subject and indirect object are the same. Examine the following sentence that uses the reflexive verb **lavarse**, and ask the questions we have used to identify subject, direct object, and indirect object:

Ellos **se** lavan las manos. *They wash their hands.*

The subject is **ellos**, since it is they *who* are doing the washing. The direct object is **las manos**, because that is *what* they wash. Those whose hands are being washed are, as the use of the reflexive pronoun **se** reveals, the same people as those doing the washing. Answering the usual questions for identifying the types of objects in this sentence proves that the reflexive is in fact a subcategory of the indirect object, which gets its own pronoun, **se**, to mark the third person singular or plural, whether or not it is followed by a direct object pronoun.

We also can change **las manos**, the direct object noun, into a direct object pronoun, **las**. When we rewrite this sentence, we create a sentence with double-object pronouns (indirect-as-reflexive followed by the direct object pronoun):

Se las lavan.	*They are washing them.*

Of course, even the English sentence, in an unconventional context, could be interpreted in various ways. Both sentences in the two examples above could be understood to mean that more than one person washes either the hands of someone else or the hands of more than one person—imagine two people having to get more than one small child cleaned up for dinner. Note, however, that for either the conventional or somewhat less common interpretation, the pronoun **se** functions to indicate to whom or for whom the action *to wash* is performed—that is, as the indirect object. Naturally, the more likely, and conventional, interpretation of this sentence (a default meaning, if you wish) is that the subject and receiver are the same person or people. Also notice the economy of **se** as the third person reflexive object pronoun: even in its function as an indirect object pronoun, it replaces **le** and **les** when these (strictly indirect object pronouns) would appear before the "l-" forms of the third person direct object pronouns.

Of course, you recognize whether **se** is used reflexively or not in just the same way as you would recognize whether **me**, **te**, **nos**, or **os** are used reflexively or as direct or indirect objects: *by observing the verb ending and taking into account the meaning of the verb.* It is easy to see which would be first interpreted (by default) as reflexive. They are the ones whose verbs have been conjugated in the third person, either singular or plural. When **se** is not used with a verb conjugated in the third person, it simply *cannot* be interpreted as a reflexive and will *always* be followed by **lo**, **la**, **los**, or **las**, revealing that **se** is replacing **le** or **les**, and therefore it is functioning as an indirect object as it is usually defined. Remember the default interpretation of **se** when the verb and **se** are both third person: **se** is being used reflexively. Only context will determine if that interpretation needs to be changed, as was seen in the example of washing children's hands. Consider the following two sets of examples using **se** and their various interpretations, which are determined by context alone, as shown by the translations of each of these minimalist sentences.

Reflexive se

Se las lava.	*He washes his hands.* *She washes her hands.* *You (formal, singular)* wash your hands.
Se las lavan.	*They wash their hands.* *They wash each other's hands.* *You (formal, plural)* wash your hands.
Se ve.	*He sees himself.* *She sees herself.* *You (formal, singular)* see yourself.
Se ven.	*They see themselves.* *They see each other.* *You (formal, plural)* see yourselves.

Indirect object se

Se las lavamos.	*We wash them (feminine plural direct object)* for him/her. *We wash them for you (formal, singular).* *We wash them for them.*
Se los lavo.	*I wash them (masculine plural direct object)* for him/her. *I wash them for you (formal, singular).* *I wash them for them.*
Se las lavas.	*You (familiar, singular)* wash them *(feminine plural direct object)* for him/her. *You wash them for them.*
Se lo laváis.	*You (familiar, plural)* wash it *(masculine singular direct object)* for him/her. *You wash it for them.*

Pseudo-passive use of se

In English, we have two principal voices: active and passive. Although Spanish also has both these voices, there is a tendency to avoid the true passive construction in favor of a **se** construction, also called the pseudo-passive. The pseudo-passive looks reflexive but makes no sense when translated as such. The lesson here is that whenever a reflexive translation of **se** makes no sense, don't try to force it—**se** is being used for some other purpose. Examine the following three examples, in which the same event is reported as active, passive, and, finally, as a pseudo-passive **se**. In order to make the type of action these sentences deal with more realistic, the past tenses are used.

Active

Los niños **rompieron** la ventana.   *The boys **broke** the window.*

Passive

La ventana **fue rota** por los niños.   *The window **was broken** by the boys.*

Pseudo-passive

Se rompió la ventana.   *The window **got broken**.*

In both English and Spanish, the active voice is straightforward and indicates the action that follows (thus the name of the tense *preterite indicative*). In this case the subject, the boys, are named as the doers of the deed, and the direct object is the window. Notice the subject-verb agreement of **niños** and **rompieron**.

The passive voice in English and in Spanish shifts the emphasis. The grammatical subject is not the real-life doer of the action, but rather the thing acted upon. In other words, the direct object of the active voice sentence, the window, becomes the subject, and the real-life subject, the boys, becomes what is known as a *passive agent* and is contained in the prepositional phrase beginning with the preposition **por** (*by*). Although the boys are still named as the ones who broke the window, the window is the focus, not the boys. Notice the subject-verb agreement of **ventana** and **fue**. The word **rota**, just as its English counterpart *broken*, is a predicate adjective and agrees in gender and number with the noun that is the subject of the sentence (**ventana**, feminine singular).

The pseudo-passive goes a step further than the true passive in that it removes the real-life subject altogether, and the grammatical subject of the verb is the window. The reflexive construction, using **se**, might make it appear that the window broke itself. The pseudo-passive, or **se** construction, is used in two common situations. First, if the real-life doer or doers of the action are not known or if the only real matter of concern is the fact at hand—the broken window. Second, and very commonly among such boys as these who broke the window, is to avoid blame. Likewise, a parent might use it to soften the blow of accusation. Adults use it to avoid finger-pointing, and so on. Notice the subject-verb agreement of **ventana** and **se rompió**. As for the English translation of the pseudo-passive, the colloquial *got-plus-predicate adjective* is often a good solution when translating from Spanish to English.

This **se** construction also is often used when an action is the main focus but a speaker wishes to show who is affected by it. This is done by using **se** followed by the indirect pronoun then the verb and is known as the *dative of interest* (*dative* being the more formal term for indirect object). In the translation of the following sentences, you'll notice that the colloquial English also employs this construction, except that there is no reflexive-seeming aspect to them. In English, some form of possessive or prepositional phrase introduced with *for* often serves the same function as the indirect object in Spanish. Some textbooks refer to this usage under the rubric of **se** with an indirect object (pointing to the person affected) for good or bad unexpected events, as these examples show:

Se me perdió el suéter.	*My sweater* **got lost**.
A Juan **se le murió** el perro.	*John's dog* **died on him**.
Se nos quemó la casa.	*Our house* **got burned**.
Se me vino a la memoria el número.	*The number* **came back** *to my mind*.
A María **se le salió** el perro a la calle.	*Mary's dog* **ran out** *into the street*.
Se te fue el dolor de cabeza.	*Your headache* **went away**.

Impersonal se

Closely related to the pseudo-passive use of **se** is the impersonal use of **se**—so close, in fact, that many textbooks do not distinguish them, because structurally they are identical. What distinguishes them is that they tend not to have to do with unexpected events, and do not lend themselves as easily to the inclusion of an indirect object to show the person or people affected. This **se** construction is commonly seen on signage and announcements of various kinds:

Se habla español aquí.	*Spanish* **spoken** *here*.
Se alquila casa.	*House* **for rent**.
Se abre a las ocho de la mañana.	**Open** *at 8 A.M.*
Se cierra a las cinco de la tarde.	**Close** *at 5 P.M.*
Se venden bicicletas.	*Bicycles* **sold**.
Se busca a Juan Fulano.	**Wanted:** *John Doe*.

With regard to subject-verb agreement in impersonal constructions, there is considerable inconsistency among Spanish speakers and writers. It is important to point out a common error among Spanish speakers in order to reassure learners that if they are aware of and observe the subject-verb agreement, they need not become insecure when they hear native speakers committing what is known by language specialists as a *native error*. While the plural is technically correct when the grammatical subject is plural, as in the example about bicycles, this agreement rule is often forgotten when the verb precedes the grammatical subject, especially in casual speech. Thus, it is possible that learners will encounter the technically incorrect form **se vende bicicletas** instead of **se venden bicicletas**. The subject-verb agreement is much more likely to be followed if the grammatical subject comes first, as in **bicicletas se venden**.

Emphatic se

As you learned in chapter 2, many verbs that are not normally reflexive, such as verbs of movement (**ir** > **irse**), other common verbs (such as **comer** > **comerse**) are made reflexive to add emphasis, but this does not change the meaning of the verb. In English, emphasis can be added to many verbs by adding prepositions (*go* > *go away*, *eat* > *eat up*). In English, these forms are known as phrasals (and by the way, cause great difficulty for Spanish speakers who are learning English).

Even though this emphatic application of the reflexive form includes all the forms of reflexive pronouns (as the examples below will help you recall, again, using the past tenses in some cases for greater realism), it is important to reiterate that **se** is seen and heard so frequently because it is the third person singular and plural of the reflexive.

Vi un tiburón y **me salí** del agua.	*I saw a shark and **flew out** of the water.*
Juan **se fue** corriendo.	*John **took off** running.*
El niño **se comió** la manzana.	*The boy **ate up** the apple.*
Los soldados **se van** a la guerra.	*The soldiers **go off** to war.*

In this chapter, both present and past tenses of verbs are used in the exercises.

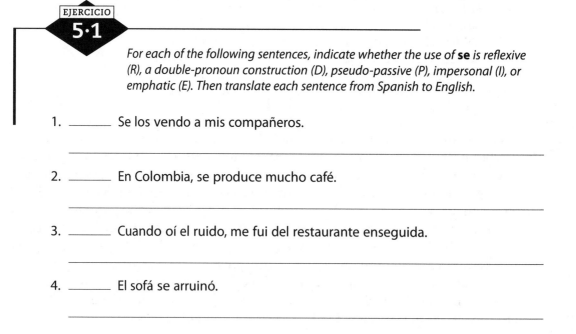

EJERCICIO
5·1

*For each of the following sentences, indicate whether the use of **se** is reflexive (R), a double-pronoun construction (D), pseudo-passive (P), impersonal (I), or emphatic (E). Then translate each sentence from Spanish to English.*

1. _____ Se los vendo a mis compañeros.

_____

2. _____ En Colombia, se produce mucho café.

_____

3. _____ Cuando oí el ruido, me fui del restaurante enseguida.

_____

4. _____ El sofá se arruinó.

_____

5. _____ Mi hermano se durmió temprano.

_____

6. _____ Se toman café y té en Seattle.

_____

7. _____ A los turistas se les acabó el dinero.

_____

8. _____ El tiempo se nos acaba.

_____

9. _____ Se buscaba a Emilio Escobar.

_____

10. _____ Se nos fue la comida por el apetito de los chicos.

_____

11. _____ Se lo regalaron a los profesores.

_____

12. _____ Se rindió el general después de la batalla.

_____

13. _____ Se dan películas francesas y españolas en ese cine.

_____

14. _____ Desde el mirador, se ve toda la ciudad.

_____

15. _____ Las vacas se comieron el maíz.

_____

Translate the following sentences from Spanish to English.

1. ¿Se te acaba el dinero a final de mes?

   _____

2. Se los van a dar mañana.

   _____

3. Pobre María, se le murió el hijo.

   _____

4. En esa calle se ofrecen muchos platos interesantes.

   _____

5. Las camisas ya se las dimos a mi mamá.

   _____

6. Se me pinchó una llanta.

   _____

7. A Juan se le apagaron las luces durante la tormenta.

   _____

8. Ese Juan no quería escucharnos y se fue gruñendo.

   _____

9. Esas ideas medievales se le subieron al cerebro y se metió a caballero andante.

   _____

10. De repente, se me ocurrió una solución al problema.

    _____

11. En Cuba se baila al son montuno.

    _____

12. Sé que se buscan novios y novias en Internet.

    _____

13. Ella se bajó la cabeza cuando le acusaron del delito.

_____

14. La computadora se me congela con frecuencia.

_____

15. Los adolescentes se comieron todos los espaguetis.

_____

16. Cuando suena el despertador, él se levanta.

_____

17. Se les escapó el conejo a los cazadores por entre la maleza.

_____

18. Cuando se es estudiante se lee mucho y se come poco.

_____

19. ¿El dinero? Juan ya se lo dio a Tomás.

_____

20. El dispositivo se dañó.

_____

EJERCICIO

5·3

Translate the following sentences from English to Spanish using **se** *constructions. There are other solutions, but concentrate on ways to deal with the meaning using* **se**.

1. The thief ran away.

_____

2. Wanted: Jesse James.

_____

3. Kathy's husband walked out on her.

_____

4. The workers fell asleep.

_____

5. Car for sale.

_____

6. She lost her purse.

_____

7. The children climbed up the tree.

_____

8. They ate up the pizza.

_____

9. The time escaped us.

_____

10. Good food is found in Acapulco.

_____

11. The door got stuck.

_____

12. The tree fell down on him.

_____

13. The idea came to them.

_____

14. Her cat died on her.

_____

15. Open at nine and close at five.

_____

16. When one is poor, one must work more.

   _____

17. Apartments for rent.

   _____

18. When the phone rings, it gets answered.

   _____

19. Her dress got ruined.

   _____

20. Spanish and French spoken here.

   _____

Pronouns as objects of prepositions

The goal of this chapter is not to study prepositions, but rather to learn what happens to certain pronouns—what forms certain pronouns need to take—when they are the objects of prepositions. It is therefore important to know what is meant by a preposition, and so we first turn our attention to prepositions in general to learn what they are, what they do, and what difficulties they present to learners. We also offer some general strategies that can be effective in mastering them. Following those observations, we examine what happens to certain pronouns when they are the object of a preposition. In fact, not much does happen, but when changes are necessary, it is essential to know what they are.

Prepositions comprise one of the nine parts of speech, together with articles, nouns, pronouns, adjectives, verbs, adverbs, conjunctions, and interjections. Compared with most of the other parts of speech, prepositions form a relatively small group of mostly one-syllable words.

The function of prepositions, in both English and Spanish, is to show the relationship between nouns or pronouns. Thus, prepositions serve as relater words. The function of prepositions when they show the relationships between nouns or pronouns with regard to time and space is rather simple.

However, prepositions can also show more complex relationships involving verbs and adjectives, and verbs and their objects. This aspect of prepositional usage usually involves learning verbs with the prepositions that can (or must) be used with them; generally, they must be learned along with verbs, one verb one at a time. The most common ones are always pointed out in standard textbooks, such as **casarse con** (*to get married to*).

The most problematic aspect of prepositional usage is the fact that the usage for a given preposition in English cannot always be adequately determined by appealing to its dictionary counterpart in Spanish.

As you venture into this territory, keep in mind that what makes prepositional usage difficult to master is the fact that several prepositions have more than one meaning in English, and that exactly which meaning it has will depend on context or, at worst, seem arbitrary. For instance, you are certainly familiar with the problems posed by two common Spanish prepositions—**por** and **para**—and know that they frequently translate into one English preposition—*for*.

Observe the following examples, noting the relationships between the highlighted prepositions, nouns, and pronouns, and observing how the prepositions mediate or determine the relationships between them in space or time. Remember that there is no apostrophe followed by the letter *-s* to show possession; instead, the preposition **de** (meaning *of* in such cases) is used to show ownership.

El **libro** está **en** la **mesa**.	The **book** is **on** the **table**.
Hay **flores alrededor de** la **casa**.	There are **flowers around** the **house**.
¿Cuántas **cajas** hay **debajo de** la **mesa**?	How many **boxes** are there **under** the **table**?
Mi **amigo** va **a Portland**.	My **friend** is going **to Portland**.
La **bicicleta** es **del niño**.	The **bicycle** is the **boy's**.
La **cena** es **después de** la **película**.	The **dinner** is **after** the **movie**.
Te doy cinco **dólares por** el **sombrero**.	I offer you five **dollars for** the **hat**.
Los **dulces** son **para ellas**.	The **candies** are **for them**.
El **bebé** está **con** su **mamá**.	The **baby** is **with** its **mother**.

The following list presents all the simple, or one-word, prepositions in Spanish. Their dictionary translations into English are given, but remember—this is but your first step to learning to use them accurately.

a	*at, to*	**hasta**	*until, to, up to*
ante	*before*	**mediante**	*by means of*
bajo	*under*	**para**	*for*
con	*with*	**por**	*for, by*
contra	*against*	**salvo**	*except, save*
de	*of, from*	**según**	*according to*
desde	*from, since*	**sin**	*without*
durante	*during*	**so**	*under (obsolete, archaic;*
en	*in, into, at, on*		*therefore found in legal*
entre	*among, between*		*documents)*
excepto	*except*	**sobre**	*on, about*
hacia	*towards*	**tras**	*after*

Of the prepositions above, **bajo** is an adjective that doubles as a preposition. Notice also that **durante, excepto, mediante,** and **salvo** are derived from the verbs **durar, exceptuar, mediar,** and **salvar.**

Spanish also has compound prepositions that are synonymous with some of the simple forms. The difference is that the compound forms tend to be *locative* (show *place* relationships) whereas the simple ones tend to be figurative and could be either temporal or spatial:

a través de	*across, through*
debajo de	*under, below*
delante de	*in front of*
detrás de	*after, behind*
encima de	*on top of, over*

There are many related compounds, often formed with adverbs-plus-prepositions. These are employed for expressing more abstract relationships, particularly those used in logical reasoning, as you can see by comparing them with their English translations. This list is offered because the translations are reliably stable and they are high-frequency phrases, although some do have more than one meaning. To help master their usage, it is recommended that advanced students write out any sentence containing compound prepositions encountered in reading or heard in speech. This will help distinguish the various situations in which one is more appropriate than another, although the dictionary meanings may be identical.

a causa de	*on account of*	**debajo de**	*under, below*
a excepción de	*with the exception of*	**debido a**	*due to*
a fuerza de	*by dint of*	**delante de**	*before* (place), *in front of*
a pesar de	*in spite of*	**dentro de**	*within*
a través de	*across, through*	**después de**	*after* (time, order)
acerca de	*about, concerning*	**detrás de**	*behind, after*
además de	*besides, in addition to*	**en cuanto a**	*as for*
adversamente a	*adversely to*	**en frente de**	*in front of*
alrededor de	*around*	**en vez de**	*instead of*
antes de	*before* (time, order)	**en virtud de**	*by virtue of*
cerca de	*near, close to*	**encima de**	*over, on top of*
con respecto a	*with respect to*	**frente a**	*opposite to, in front of*
con tal de	*provided*	**junto a**	*next to, close to*
concerniente a	*concerning*	**lejos de**	*far from*
conforme a	*according to*	**por causa de**	*on account of*
congruente a	*consistent with*	**por razón de**	*by reason of*
contrario a	*contrary to*	**relativo a**	*in relation to*
correspondiente a	*corresponding to*	**sin embargo**	*notwithstanding*

Having examined prepositions generally, learners may now more easily appreciate what is meant when it is observed that a pronoun is the object of a preposition. We will now examine what forms pronouns take when they are in this grammatical situation.

We have already seen one use of pronouns as objects of prepositions when we examined clarifiers or emphatic (when they appear redundant) forms for the indirect and reflexive object pronouns. Examine the following sentences. The use of **mismo, mismos, misma,** and **mismas** is illustrated merely in its role as a commonly used adjective that emphasizes either a reflexive or even an indirect object:

Juan **se** los da **a ella misma.**	*John gives them right **to her.***
Te lo doy **a ti.**	*I give it **to you.***
Ellos **me** lo dan **a mí.**	*They give it **to me.***
Juan **se** paga primero **a sí mismo.**	*John pays **himself** first.*
Ellos **nos** lo envían **a nosotros.**	*They send it **to us.***

When a pronoun is the object of a preposition, it assumes what is formally known as the *prepositional case.* At the beginning of this chapter, it was observed that not much happens to the pronouns when they are objects of prepositions, but there are some essential changes. So finally, here is the fortunate news you have been expecting:

The object of preposition forms of pronouns are the same as the subject forms—*except* for the *first* and *second persons singular* (**mí, ti**) and the *reflexive object pronoun of the third person, singular and plural* (**sí**). The most conspicuous additional rule is that learners also must remember that when **mí, ti,** or **sí** (*myself, yourself,* or *your/him/herself*) are used with **con** (*with*), the forms are **conmigo** (*with me*), **contigo** (*with you*), and **consigo** (*with himself, herself, yourself*—singular or plural—or *themselves*).

Noting these special cases—**conmigo, contigo,** and the use of **sí** as the third person singular and plural reflexive pronoun—the following list shows all the possible forms of pronouns arranged by person and number:

mí, conmigo	**nosotros, -as**
ti, contigo	**vosotros, -as**
él, sí, consigo	**ellos, sí, consigo**
ella, sí, consigo	**ellas, sí, consigo**
usted, sí, consigo	**ustedes, sí, consigo**

One final observation: mere accompaniment is not expressed in the same way as the reflexive. Compare the following examples, noting that in the examples that have both third person subjects and objects, the use of **consigo** makes it clear that the action is reflexive, while the subject forms of the third person, used as objects of the preposition, make it clear that the subject is accompanied by someone other than him- or herself:

Quiero ir **contigo.**	*I want to go **with you.***
Ellos **se** lo llevan **consigo.**	*They are taking it **with them.***

Lo tengo **conmigo**.	*I have it **with me**.*
Theresa va **con ella**.	*Theresa is going **with her**.*
Juan come **con él**.	*John eats **with him**.*
Él se sienta **con Ud**.	*He sits down **with you**.*
Él habla **consigo** mismo.	*He talks **to himself**.*

The last two examples are useful for clarifying the rule stated above. In the next-to-last example, the verb **sentarse** is reflexive, as it must be (one sits *oneself* down), but the person with whom the subject is sitting is not the subject (**Él**), but rather the person to whom one is speaking (**Ud.**). In like manner, all third person objects of prepositions will simply be the subject forms, unless that object is reflexive. As for the singular forms of the first and second person (familiar, or **tú** form), they always take the objective forms **mí**, **ti**, or, when following **con**, **conmigo** and **contigo**, respectively.

One further exception is a bit of a reversal of the rule. The prepositions **entre, excepto,** and **según** (and, as a reminder, the adverb **como**—when it means *since* or *as*) are always followed by the *subject* forms, even for the first and second persons singular.

Entre tú y yo, esto no es tan difícil como parece.	***Between you and me**, this isn't as difficult as it seems.*
¿**Según** quién, me preguntas? Pues, **según yo**.	*According to whom, you ask? Well, **according to me**.*
Todos mis amigos vinieron, **excepto tú**.	*All my friends came, **except you**.*

EJERCICIO 6·1

Circle the proper form of the pronoun to serve as the object of the preposition.

1. El maestro está detrás de (yo/me/mí/conmigo).

2. Su mamá va a la tienda con (tú/te/ti/-tigo).

3. Mis amigos vienen de la casa de (Ud./le/lo/se/consigo).

4. Éste es un asunto personal entre (tú/te/ti) y (yo/me/mí).

5. Sus enemigos hacen una campaña contra (él/lo/le/se).

6. Yo tengo un postre delicioso para (tú/te/ti).

7. Las animadoras corren hacia (ellos/se/les/los).

8. Romeo no quiere a nadie excepto a (ella/la/le/se).

9. Julieta no ama a nadie salvo a (él/lo/le/se).

10. Juan es un poco loco; siempre habla con (él/lo/le/-sigo).

11. Pepe, según (tú/te/ti), ¿cuál es la respuesta correcta?

12. Maestra, según (yo/me/mí), se debe usar la forma del sujeto en estas últimas dos.

13. Bueno, como (yo/me/mí) no tengo la menor idea, confío en tu opinión.

14. Ella lo dice delante de (tú/te/ti).

15. Los estudiantes se ponen enfrente de (él/le/lo/se).

16. La verdad, mi amor, es que no puedo vivir sin (tú/te/ti).

17. Los niños se llevan los dulces con (ellos/se/sí/-sigo).

18. Ella es tan alta como (tú/te/ti).

19. No voy a hablar con (ella/le/la/se).

20. Ella no va a hablar con (yo/me/mí/-migo).

EJERCICIO

6·2

Translate the following sentences from Spanish to English.

1. No queremos hablar con él.

   _____

2. Según ellos, no hay calentamiento global.

   _____

3. Frente a ella, se ve un rascacielos.

   _____

4. Juan lo tiene escondido, detrás de sí.

   _____

5. ¿Desean ellas ir a la playa con Ud.?

   _____

6. Entre él y ella, siempre hay paz y armonía.

_____

7. Yo prefiero la camisa que está detrás de ti.

_____

8. Ella va a discutirlo contigo.

_____

9. Creo que este regalo es para ti.

_____

10. Delante de ellos, ella le declaró su amor.

_____

11. Detrás de Ud., hay un monumento importante.

_____

12. Teresa se lo lleva consigo.

_____

13. No hay disputas entre ellos.

_____

14. El criminal comparece ante él.

_____

15. Si te vas, van a ir tras de ti.

_____

16. Juana y Tomás se lo llevan consigo.

_____

17. La opinión contraria es de ti, no de mí.

_____

18. Ella quiere escalar la montaña contigo.

_____

19. A causa de mí, se arruinó el pastel.

_____

20. Juan está enfermo, entonces vamos a hacerlo por él.

_____

Translate the following sentences from English to Spanish.

1. They want to go with you (*familiar, singular*).

_____

2. She is behind him.

_____

3. I am against them.

_____

4. She is talking to herself.

_____

5. They are in front of you (*formal, plural*).

_____

6. Is she going to come with you (*formal, singular*)?

_____

7. According to him, there is no problem.

_____

8. On account of you (*familiar, singular*), I am happy.

_____

9. For you (*familiar, singular*), I would give the world.

_____

10. Without her, John is sad.

_____

11. They leave the building, following them.

_____

12. Are you (*familiar, singular*) going to the movies with me?

_____

13. There is no one for me except for her.

_____

14. He is solving the problem without us.

_____

15. I want to live my life next to you (*familiar, singular*).

_____

16. She wants to live her life next to me.

_____

17. I don't know how she can live without me.

_____

18. The boss has fifty people under him.

_____

19. They don't talk about you (*formal, singular*).

_____

20. Besides you (*familiar, singular*), five people are coming tomorrow.

_____

Demonstrative, possessive, and interrogative pronouns

The names of these three categories of pronouns clearly reveal their respective functions. The *demonstrative* pronouns point out or indicate something, much like when you point your finger toward something to show your listener. The *possessive* pronouns show to whom something belongs. Finally, the *interrogative* pronouns seek to find out the identity of a subject or object. In all three cases, since these are pronouns, they replace some generic category of noun that has been previously stated or that is somehow otherwise implicit. Observe the examples in the following three sections and note how—often without further context—it is possible to tell for sure only the gender and number of the noun the pronoun has replaced.

Demonstrative pronouns

Ésta es la mejor camisa.	*This is the best shirt.*
Prefiero ver **aquélla**.	*I prefer to see **that one**.*
Ése es el más guapo.	*That one is the most handsome.*
¿No te gustan **éstas**?	*Don't you like **these**?*

In the first example, it is clear that two people are comparing shirts, but had the word **camisa** been omitted from the Spanish (and the word *shirt* from the English translation), it would have been impossible for an eavesdropper on the conversation to know anything more than that the two people were comparing one feminine singular item with another.

Of course, it is possible to make some probable guesses as to what **aquélla** and **ése** refer to, but not with absolute certainty. It seems likely that **aquélla** means a *movie* (**película**), but it could just as well be a *magazine* (**revista**) or any other feminine singular object, including a female person or animal for which a separate term exists (**mujer**, **gallina**). Likewise, **ése** seems to refer to a *man* (**hombre**), but it could just as likely be a *horse* (**caballo**) or even a *suit* (**traje**). Only context would solve the lack of specificity.

In form, the demonstrative pronouns are identical to the demonstrative adjectives, except that the pronouns bear a written accent. In terms of usage, the demonstrative adjective always precedes the noun it modifies and agrees with it in gender and number. The demonstrative pronouns, as the preceding examples show, agree in like manner with the noun they replace.

Demonstrative adjectives

MASCULINE	FEMININE	
este, estos	esta, estas	*this, these*
ese, esos	esa, esas	*that, those*
aquel, aquellos	aquella, aquellas	*that, those*

Demonstrative pronouns

MASCULINE	FEMININE	
éste, éstos	ésta, éstas	*this, these*
ése, ésos	ésa, ésas	*that, those*
aquél, aquéllos	aquélla, aquéllas	*that, those*

The translations for the demonstrative pronouns correspond to such English expressions as *this one, that one, those over there,* and so forth. As learners work with demonstratives, both adjectives and pronouns, they also must keep in mind two other things. First, since the concept of the distance of a thing is relative to the speaker's point of view, just how far away a thing has to be before one says, for instance, *this shirt* or *that shirt,* is itself relative and therefore quite flexible, just as it is in English. Second, Spanish has a third distance, as shown by **aquel** and its corresponding forms, which is used when the distance is most remote from the speaker. It is similar to southern United States expressions of distance that employ the word *yonder.*

Possessive pronouns

La bicicleta es **mía**.	*The bicycle is **mine**.*
¿Es **suyo** el perro?	*Is the dog **yours/his/hers** (or yours—plural)?*
Allí se ve la **nuestra**.	*There you can see **ours**.*
El libro es **tuyo**, ¿no?	*The book is **yours**, isn't it?*

Possessive pronouns are also known as *intensive* or *emphatic* forms, used instead of a simple possessive adjective. Compare the sentences above with the following, which use the possessive *adjectives* instead of the possessive *pronouns*. Of course, in order to rewrite the sentences, the noun has to be supplied. The fact of ownership is indicated by the possessive adjective that precedes the noun:

Es **mi** bicicleta.	*It's **my** bicycle.*
Es **su** perro.	*It's **your/his/her** (or *your*—plural) dog.*
Allí se ve **nuestra** casa.	*There one can see **our** house.*
Es **tu** libro, ¿no?	*It's **your** book, isn't it?*

One of the biggest challenges in using possessive pronouns is to keep in mind the gender and number of the noun possessed, and to not confuse them with the gender and number of the possessor. In the first example of the possessive pronouns on page 76, **bicicleta** is feminine singular; thus, regardless of the gender or number of the owner (supposing two people could own one bicycle between them), the form of the possessive pronoun must agree with it—in this case, **mía**.

The forms of all the possessive pronouns are given below. Note how English often has only one corresponding form, whereas Spanish, with the need for gender and number agreement, has four. Additionally, the third person forms can refer to many owners, and one set is used for both singular and plural:

Singular owner

MASCULINE	FEMININE	
mío, míos	**mía, mías**	*mine*
tuyo, tuyos	**tuya, tuyas**	*yours* (familiar)
suyo, suyos	**suya, suyas**	*his, hers, yours* (formal)

Plural owner

MASCULINE	FEMININE	
nuestro, nuestros	**nuestra, nuestras**	*ours*
vuestro, vuestros	**vuestra, vuestras**	*yours* (familiar)
suyo, suyos	**suya, suyas**	*theirs, yours* (formal)

The best way to internalize the application of gender and number agreement when using possessive pronouns before trying one's knowledge in the exercises is to examine some strongly contrasted examples. The first example that follows shows how a plurality of owners is reflected by the root **nuestr-**, and the gender and number of the item owned (in this case, a house) is shown by the feminine singular ending. The other two examples each have singular owners, one male and one female (as shown by the names), who each own a plurality of items whose gender is opposite to their own biological gender. For intermediate and advanced students the concept of agreement is nothing new, but by isolating it in the context of possessive pronouns, you can eliminate any residual hesitation you might have.

¿La casa? Es **nuestra**.	*The house? It's **ours**.*
Teresa, ¿es **tuyo** el libro?	*Theresa, is the book **yours**?*
Juan, ¿es **tuya** la camisa?	*John, is the shirt **yours**?*

Interrogative pronouns

Interrogative words are those words used to ask questions and, thus, to elicit information. Interrogative pronouns form a subclass of the more general category of interrogative words. Interrogatives are identical in form to relative pronouns, which we will consider separately, except that the interrogatives bear a written accent.

Many interrogative words are adverbs (**¿cuándo?**, **¿cómo?**, **¿dónde?** etc.) and seek to find out such information as *when*, *how*, and *where*, but this chapter focuses strictly on those question words that are meant to elicit a *noun* as a response. Interrogative pronouns are words used to introduce a question, the purpose of which is to find out the identity of someone or something, whether this person or thing is real (*girl*, *book*) or an abstraction (*love*, *honesty*).

¿Qué es esto?	*What is this?*
¿Quién es tu actor favorito?	*Who is your favorite actor?*
¿Qué sabores de helado te gustan más?	*Which are your favorite ice cream flavors?*
¿Cuál te gusta más?	*Which one do you like the most?*

Strictly speaking, only **¿quién?** (*who?*) and **¿quiénes?** (*who?*—used when the expected reply is plural) are interrogative pronouns. The interrogative pronoun **¿quién?**, and its plural form **¿quiénes?**, can refer only to a human being or beings; **¿qué?** and **¿cuáles?** can refer to people, things, or abstractions. The other interrogatives we include are interrogative *adjectives*, which are also often used to ask questions whose expected answer is a noun (the adjectives are *substantivized*; that is, they become pronouns): **¿qué?** (*what?*) and **¿cuál?** (*which?*), and **¿cuáles?** (*which ones?*—used when the expected response is plural). All of these also form compound interrogatives when preceded by prepositions, such as **¿de quién?**, **¿con quién?**, and so forth.

Match the nouns on the left with the proper demonstrative pronouns from the list on the right.

1. _____ flores cerca de la mesa
2. _____ revista a tu lado
3. _____ sillas aquí
4. _____ señorita a mi lado
5. _____ asientos en la otra tienda
6. _____ chico allá
7. _____ casas al otro lado de la ciudad
8. _____ muchachos cerca del bar
9. _____ niños aquí
10. _____ maestra en la otra escuela
11. _____ libro que tengo en la mano
12. _____ edificio al fondo de la calle

a. ése
b. aquéllas
c. éste
d. ésta
e. esos
f. éstos
g. éstas
h. aquél
i. aquélla
j. aquéllos
k. ésa
l. ésas

Select the possessive pronouns on the right that properly complete the phrases on the left.

1. Juanito, te la regalo; la camisa ya es _____.
2. Digo que ese carro es _____ y no de él.
3. Vivimos en una casa. Es _____.
4. Amigo, las camisas son _____.
5. Somos una familia rica. Las casas son _____.
6. La billetera es de mi hermano. Es _____.

a. mío.
b. suya
c. mías
d. tuyos
e. suyas
f. nuestras

7. Compré estas tierras y ya son _____ .

g. tuya

8. Queremos al perro. Es _____ .

h. mía

9. Jaimito, ¿son _____ todos estos relojes?

i. nuestro

10. ¡No hice nada! La culpa no es _____ .

j. tuyas

11. Este libro es del profesor. Es _____ .

k. nuestra

12. Estas blusas son de la señora. Son _____ .

l. suyo

EJERCICIO
7·3

Fill in the blanks with the proper demonstrative, possessive, or interrogative pronouns.

Mi amiga Teresa trabaja en una tienda de ropa en el centro de la ciudad. No trabaja

en (1) _____ que está al lado del restaurante Xochimilco, sino en la que

está cerca de la catedral. Todos los días, las clientes, muchas de ellas amigas de ella y

(2) _____ también, entran y le hacen preguntas.

　　—Hola Teresa, pero, ¿no tienen otra blusa parecida a (3) _____ ?

　　—¿Cuál? Ah, (4) _____ de color rosado. Claro, Maritere. Mira...

(5) _____ que está allí, en la ventana, de color azul. ¿Para

(6) _____ es?

　　—Es para mi amiga Elena.

　　—¡No me digas! ¿(7) _____ muchacha rubia que sale con Andrés?

　　—(8) _____ misma. Oye, ¿(9) _____ de estas dos crees

que le quedaría mejor, la azul o (10) _____ , la rosada?

—Pues, (11) _____, aquí... la azul. Sabes, mi color es rosado, pero el

(12) _____, digo de Elena, definitivamente es azul. Hace juego con sus

ojos. En cambio, los (13) _____ son castaños y por eso yo prefiero los

colores más cálidos.

—Bueno, Maritere, y sobre el tema de la boda de Elena, ¿dónde será la

recepción? ¿En el hotel Buenavista o en...?

—(14) _____ que está más allá de la avenida Revolución, cerca del

mar, ¿cómo se llama? Se me olvida.

—Las Brisas, Maritere. He oído decir que es bueno, pero no sé mucho de él.

¿(15) _____ tipo de hotel es?

—De cinco estrellas, por supuesto. A Elena no le gustan esos hoteles a este lado

del malecón. Yo sé que también estás invitada. ¿Vas con tu novio o no?

—Lamentablemente no. Rompimos hace dos meses, así que creo que voy sola.

—¡Ni hablar, Teresa! Vas a ir conmigo porque no tengo novio y hace tiempo que

las dos nos hemos hecho buenas amigas y somos amigas de Elena.

Relative pronouns

The study of relative pronouns is very closely linked to the study of interrogative pronouns whose forms they share, but without a written accent. In terms of grammatical function, relative pronouns can be either subjects or objects.

The function of a relative pronoun is to refer back to a previously mentioned noun, called its *antecedent*, which may be either a subject or an object of the relative clause. Generally speaking, a relative pronoun performs the role of the conjunction *and*, followed by a personal or demonstrative pronoun. Compare the following two versions of an English sentence:

> *John gave me two guppies **that** reproduced quickly.*
> *John gave me two guppies, **and they** reproduced quickly.*

In the above sentences, guppies are the direct object of the verb *to give*. However, only the first sentence has a relative clause, introduced by the relative pronoun *that*. This relative pronoun is understood to stand in for the guppies (the antecedent). The second sentence is simply a compound sentence—two sentences made one by the use of *and*.

In the following English sentences, the words *that* and *whom* (used for people only, in more formal usage) are employed to introduce relative clauses whose antecedents become direct objects. Once again, the possible reconstruction of the sentences shows how the equivalent of the relative is *and + personal pronoun*. Note how the relative clauses in which the subjects (*cars, children*) become objects are sandwiched between the subjects and the verbs (*are, play*). We will see this same structural feature in Spanish sentences in a moment.

> *The cars **that** we bought are good.*
> *We bought cars, **and they** are good.*
> *The children **whom** we teach play a lot.*
> *We teach children, **and they** play a lot.*

Turning now to Spanish, there are only five relative pronouns in common usage (**cuyo**, **cuyos**, **cuya**, and **cuyas**—all meaning *whose*—are so uncommon in speech and encountered less and less frequently even in writing that this pronoun is nearly obsolete). If you don't count the plurals of two of them as separate forms, there are only three:

que	*that, who, whom*
quien, quienes	*who*
cual, cuales	*which*

Most students of Spanish quickly realize how common the word **que** is. Since this word is invariable in form and can be used in so many ways, a brief aside is in order, to review some of its more common uses. Besides being a relative pronoun, just as its English translation *that*, it can serve as a conjunction linking two clauses. In English, the conjunction *that* is often omitted, but it cannot be in Spanish:

Espero **que** tú puedas venir.	*I hope **that** you can come.*
	I hope you can come.
Pensé **que** habías llegado.	*I thought **that** you had arrived.*
	I thought you had arrived.

Sometimes **que** is untranslatable (as in the verb phrase **tener** + **que** + infinitive, *to have to . . .*). This little powerhouse of a word also is used in quite a formulaic way to form comparatives, when it is translated as *than*:

Mi casa es más grande **que** la tuya.	*My house is bigger **than** yours.*

As a relative pronoun, **que** is the most commonly used in both speaking and writing. It can refer back to a previously mentioned person or thing. It can be the subject or object of the relative clause. Keep in mind that when **que** is used to refer to people, it should never be preceded by a preposition, not even the personal **a**, but when it refers to things as direct objects, it can, and often must be preceded by a preposition.

Que as subject of the relative clause

El niño **que** estudia mucho es Juanito.	*The boy **who** studies a lot is Johnny.*
Los libros **que** cayeron son costosos.	*The books **that** fell are expensive.*

Que as object of the relative clause

El niño **que** veo es muy inteligente.	*The boy **that** I see is very intelligent.*
La leche **que** compramos está estropeada.	*The milk **that** we bought is spoiled.*
La casa **que** veo es grande.	*The house **that** I see is large.*

Whenever a preposition is used with a relative pronoun, it must precede it. The English usage of placing a preposition at the end of a relative clause is absolutely forbidden in Spanish.

El hombre **de quien** te hablé, es rico.	*The man **whom** I told you **about** is rich.*
El país **en que** vivimos es grande.	*The country **that** we live **in** is big.*
El cuchillo **con que** trabajo es afilado.	*The knife **that** I work **with** is sharp.*

As the first example above exemplifies, the relative pronoun **quien**, along with its plural **quienes**, can refer only to human beings—unlike **que**, which can refer equally to people or things. **Quien** and **quienes** should be used when a person (or people) is the object of the relative clause, and always if a preposition precedes the relative pronoun. When no preposition is needed, the use of **quien** or **quienes** rather than **que** to refer to people is a matter of formality, **quien** and **quienes** being more elevated in style.

The first sentence below is an example of when either **que** or **quien** is acceptable; the second shows how the *personal* **a** (or any other needed preposition) is used with **quien**. The third sentence is an example of a situation in which **que** would not be admissible, since the preposition **con** is needed; the same rule about placing the preposition before the relative pronoun is observed. Note that this third sentence also has two possible translations into English, the second being more formal.

El hombre **que** veo es fuerte.	*The man **that** I see is strong.*
El hombre **a quien** veo es fuerte.	*The man **whom** I see is strong.*
El hombre **con quien** hablé es mi padre.	*The man **that** I talked **to** is my father.*
	*The man **with whom** I spoke is my father.*

Another observation about **quien** is that it also is used in what may be regarded as proverbial style, as in the English "he who . . ." A couple of examples of proverbs should suffice to get the feel for this somewhat archaic or formulaic usage of **quien**.

Quien tiene padrino se bautiza.	***He who** has a godfather gets baptized.*
Quien bajo buen árbol se arrima, buena sombra le cobija.	***He who** stands under a big tree is protected by a big shadow.*

Finally, **que** and **quien** can be used to distinguish between two otherwise possible antecedents, one a person and one a thing, as the following examples show:

La dueña del carro, **que** está en malas condiciones, me pidió que lo arreglara.	*The owner of the car, **that** is in bad condition, asked me to fix it.*
La dueña del carro, **quien** está en el hospital, me pidió que lo cuidara.	*The owner of the car, **who** is in the hospital, asked me to watch it for her.*

As all learners of the language quickly discover, Spanish is a language that depends heavily on gender and number agreement. While at first this is a stumbling block for English speakers, for whom the concept of grammatical gender is unfamiliar, they may be glad to learn that Spanish also takes great advantage of this feature; it allows for greater clarity when using relative pronouns than in English, where the proper antecedent might remain ambiguous.

The further specification is accomplished by the use of the articles **el**, **los**, **la**, or **las** before either **que** or **cual** (or **cuales**, in the case of **los** or **las**). As the following examples show, the addition of these articles gives Spanish even more capacity to distinguish between possible antecedents than even the difference between **que** and **quien**, which, as already noted, is limited to allowing a distinction only between a human and nonhuman antecedent. These further distinctions become necessary—and are made possible by the use of the articles—if there are two possible antecedents in the main clause to which the relative pronoun refers, and when the difference in gender or number permits the relative pronoun to be further specified to refer to only one. In the examples, both the antecedents and the relative pronouns (and any associated preposition) are set in boldface, to show the precision made possible by the use of the articles in addition to the relative pronouns. The use of **lo cual** (or equally **lo que**) in the last example is a reminder that the neuter form of **lo** refers to something indefinite, a general idea.

Mi amigo me dio **un mapa** para llegar al pueblo, **sin el cual** me habría sido imposible hallar el camino.	*My friend gave me **a map** to find the town, **without which** it would have been impossible for me to find my way.*
Mi amigo me dio direcciones para llegar al **pueblo**, **el cual** no quedaba lejos de la ciudad.	*My friend gave me directions to find the **town**, **which** wasn't far from the city.*
Mi amigo me dio **direcciones** para llegar al pueblo, **las cuales** eran muy confusas.	*My friend gave me **directions** to find the town, **which** were very confusing.*
El profesor nos indicó **mucho** sobre la teoría, **lo cual** nos ayudó al tomar el examen.	*The professor told us **a lot** about the theory, **which** helped us when we took the test.*

A final observation about using **el que** or **el cual** (and all the other forms): the choice is a matter of style. The use of **el cual**, **los cuales**, and so forth is more formal and found more often in writing than in speech. The above examples would also be correct, albeit more conversational, by substituting **que** for **cual** or **cuales**.

Fill in the blank using **que**, **quien**, *or* **quienes** *according to whether the antecedent is a thing or a person (or people).*

1. Compramos un nuevo carro para nuestro hijo, a _____ le gustó mucho.

2. El carro _____ compramos le gustó a nuestro hijo.

3. Fuimos a las montañas _____ están cerca de la costa.

4. Les escribí a todas las señoritas con _____ bailé en la boda de mi tío.

5. Oye, mi amor, ¿es ésta la carta de _____ me hablaste el otro día?

6. Fueron al zoológico todos los alumnos a _____ hablamos ayer.

7. Los policías a _____ vimos enfrente del banco desaparecieron antes del robo.

8. La casa de mi abuelo, _____ está al otro lado del pueblo, es muy original.

9. Los muchachos para _____ escribimos recomendaciones, fueron bien recibidos.

10. Las hijas del Sr. Gómez, _____ recibieron becas, quieren ser astronautas.

11. El perro _____ vi no tenía una estrella en la frente.

12. Los estudiantes de lenguas necesitan personas con _____ puedan practicar.

13. Después de la fiesta _____ le dieron sus padres, Belisa se durmió.

14. Salí de la casa cuando vi al hombre _____ me había llamado el día anterior.

15. Los chicos _____ no pierden tiempo con los videojuegos tendrán éxito en la vida.

Fill in the blank with the proper form of **el cual**, **la cual**, **los cuales**, **las cuales**, or **lo cual**, *according to the antecedent.*

1. Compramos un auto, _____ pronto tuvo problemas con la transmisión.

2. No quise castigar a los niños, _____ se alegraron al saberlo.

3. Mi hermana decidió echar las revistas, _____ habían estado en su cuarto por meses.

4. Juan salió a dar de comer a los animales, _____ corrieron hacia él cuando lo vieron.

5. Llamaron a los mejores profesores, _____ no sabían qué decir.

6. Las hijas del Sr. Gómez, todas _____ recibieron becas, quieren ser astronautas.

7. Celebraban las obras de los artistas más distinguidos, _____ hacía tiempo que habían muerto, por supuesto.

8. El cazador disparó al pájaro, _____ voló por entre la maleza y se salvó.

9. Los inquisidores quemaron el libro, _____ inspiró a que más gente lo leyera.

10. Hicieron mejoras en su computadora, _____ le agradó mucho a María.

11. Juan limpió la fotocopiadora con descuido, _____ se dañó pronto después.

12. El carpintero reparó los muebles muy bien, _____ luego logró vender por un buen precio.

13. El sastre cortó el paño para hacer unos pantalones, _____ me quedaron bien.

14. Ese chico no obedece a sus padres, _____ le va a causar problemas cuando sea adolescente.

15. Los niños jugaban con la lámpara de aceite, _____ se rompió, incendiando la casa.

Translate the following sentences from Spanish to English.

1. Veo el sol que nos alumbra con sus rayos.

_____

2. Cuando escuché lo que ella había hecho, me enojé.

_____

3. Tengo varios discos de los años 50, los cuales me parecen ridículos ahora.

_____

4. Los caballos salieron en estampida del corral, mientras que los vaqueros, quienes los deberían haber perseguido, parecían no saber qué hacer.

_____

5. El tren que salió temprano tuvo un problema mecánico dos horas después.

_____

6. Había muchos árboles en el jardín del Sr. Salazar, quien decidió dejar sólo tres.

_____

7. Había tantos árboles en el jardín del Sr. Salazar que él decidió cortarlos.

_____

8. Hay tantos políticos que nos mienten tanto que no se les puede creer.

_____

9. Los autores de las novelas de quienes me habló el poeta murieron muy jóvenes.

_____

10. A causa de la tuberculosis, los novelistas que escribieron en el siglo xix no vivían muchos años generalmente.

_____

Translate the following sentences from English to Spanish using the proper relative pronouns. Be careful with the placement of prepositions!

1. We soon will see our aunt who lives in Seattle.

   _____

2. The house is very beautiful, for those who like that style.

   _____

3. There are a lot of things in the world that need our attention.

   _____

4. Is this the book I told you about?

   _____

5. Is that the guy you (*familiar, singular*) went out with last week?

   _____

6. These are the children we bought presents for.

   _____

7. This is the gun he shot the bear with.

   _____

8. The pens on the desk, which are expensive, were gifts.

   _____

9. Is she the girl you got the phone call from?

   _____

10. The king likes to play games, which is a good thing.

   _____

Indefinite pronouns

As the name suggests, an indefinite pronoun is a word that stands in for some noun that refers to someone or something vague or nonspecific. A few English examples will suffice to begin our examination of this last category of commonly used Spanish pronouns: *something, nothing, someone, nobody*, etc. The contrastive nature (positive and negative) of these indefinite pronouns also is found in Spanish.

Just as English has a need for this small set of pronouns, Spanish too has a short list of similar words. Unlike proper English, in which double negatives are absolutely wrong, double negatives are *required* in Spanish when a negative indefinite pronoun is involved, such as **nadie** (*nobody* or *no one*) if, in the first part of the sentence, **no** is used. Observe the following contrastive examples of positive and negative indefinite pronouns. Note that in English one needs to use only one negative when the pronoun refers to *nothing* or *no one*, whereas Spanish rigorously uses a double-negative construction:

Veo a **alguien** en la ventana.	*I see **someone** in the window.*
No veo a **nadie** en la ventana.	*I don't see **anyone** in the window.*
Hay **algo** en la mesa.	*There is **something** on the table.*
No hay **nada** en la mesa.	*There is **nothing** on the table.*

Of course, the word *nobody* is often used in English, but only if no other negative word is used, such as *no*, either alone or contracted as in *don't*—see the examples below. In Spanish, if the sentence does not lead with **no**, then the negative indefinite pronoun moves toward the front of the sentence, as the subject pronoun. This structure is somewhat unusual in Spanish and is reserved for a rhetorical flourish of emphasis.

Nadie está en la ventana.	*Nobody is at the window.*
Nada hay en la mesa.	*There is **nothing** on the table.*

Let's now examine the full list of such pronouns in Spanish. We must also include in this list those indefinite adjectives that can be substantivized—that is, that become pronouns when the noun or nouns they refer to have been previously mentioned or are otherwise understood. The translations offered are in some cases inadequate, given the rhetorical contexts in which some of them are used.

algo	*something*	**nada**	*nothing*
alguien	*someone*	**nadie**	*no one, nobody*
alguno	*some*	**ninguno**	*none, not any*
bastante	*plenty, lots*	**poco**	*a little*
cuál	*some* (used correlatively)	**quién**	*he who, one who, who so*
cualquiera	*anyone*	**quienquiera**	*whoever, whosoever*
demasiado	*too much*	**tal**	*such a one*
harto	*much too much, far too much*	**todo**	*everything, all the—*
		uno	*one*
mucho	*much, a lot, lots*		

Examining the words in the list above, we first note that only **alguien**, **nadie**, **quien**, and **quienquiera** are pronouns that can refer to people *only*. On the other hand, **algo** and **nada** can stand in only for a thing and are singular. When they are used in such a way that the speaker could mean a collection of stuff, then they are collective singulars, which means that if they are the subject of a verb, that verb will have to be third person singular. Compare the following two examples. In the first sentence, **algo** is the direct object; in the second, it is the subject:

Veo **algo** en la mesa.	*I see **something** on the table.*
Algo tiene que suceder pronto.	***Something** has to happen soon.*

Because they are indefinite pronouns, **alguien**, **nadie**, **algo**, and **nada** are invariable in form; that is, they represent someone or something whose gender is at the moment unknown. As the two sentences above show, they have no plural form per se, and when they are the subject of a verb, the verb is conjugated in the third person singular.

The number **uno** is a pronoun when its meaning is the impersonal English *one*—a person in the abstract, indefinite, or general sense. It is very close in meaning to, and often used instead of, an impersonal **se** construction. The common interrogatives **cuál**, **quién**, and **tal** (a common adjective uncommonly used as a pronoun) are used as indefinite pronouns in certain formulaic constructions. Examine the following sentences:

Uno nunca puede saber el futuro.	***One** can never know the future.*
No **se puede** saber el futuro.	***One** can never know the future.*
Todos, **cuál** más, **cuál** menos, estaban a favor.	*All, **some** more, **some** less, were in favor.*
Tal hay que estará de acuerdo con él.	*There may be **such who** agree with him.*

The adjectives **alguno** and **ninguno**, in all their gender and number variations, become pronouns when used alone to refer to people or things. The same is true of the neuter forms **bastante**, **demasiado**, **harto**, **mucho**, and **todo**, when they refer to some abstraction. Of these, **harto** is somewhat in disuse, and in some regions (Puerto Rico comes to mind), it is generally used as an allusion to an obscenity (meaning *full of . . .*). When they function as pronouns, of course, they can be subjects or objects, as several of the examples show. Learners are also encouraged to consider the subtle difference between **bastante** and **suficiente**, which is an adjective that can sometimes be substantivized. When **bastante** is used (either as an adjective or as a pronoun), it implies an overabundance. When **suficiente** is used it means at least *just enough*, but not more than enough.

Alguno hay por aquí.	*There is **some** around here.*
No encuentro **ninguno**.	*I can't find **any**.*
Bastante dijo para que lo entendamos.	***Enough** was said by him that we understand.*
Demasiado se ha dicho.	***Too much** has been said.*
Juan ha dicho **demasiado**.	*John has said **too much**.*
Harto ha comido.	*He has eaten **much too much**.*
Mucho ha pasado en ese país.	***Much** has happened in that country.*
Tiene **mucho** que contarnos.	*He has **much** to tell us.*
Todo lo que él dijo es verdad.	***All** that he said is true.*
Nos contó **todo**.	*He told us **all**.*

Some general observations are in order regarding **quienquiera** and **cualquiera**. It should be easy to see that both of these words are compounds of **quien** and **cual** combined with the third person singular present subjunctive of the verb **querer**. Interestingly, they are invariable in form and are used when referring to masculine or feminine nouns. Their plural forms are **cualesquier**, **cualesquiera**, and **quienesquiera**—all of which are so rarely used as to be nearly obsolete, but readers will encounter them even today in formal writing.

Both these words express indifference or lack of distinction of one or more people or things within a group. When placed before or after a noun, **cualquiera** is adjectival; it drops the final -**a** when used before a noun but retains it if it follows one. If placed after a noun, the noun is preceded by an article or demonstrative adjective, as these two sentences, using **cualquiera** as an adjective, show:

Cualquier idea suya será tonta.	*Any idea of his will be stupid.*
Una idea **cualquiera** le basta.	*Any old idea is good enough for him.*

Cualquiera only becomes a pronoun (i.e., substantivizes) when it is used without a noun, as can happen with demonstrative adjectives. Likewise, the noun or nouns that **cualquier** (and all its other forms) represents in such cases is understood or previously mentioned. When used in an exclamatory sentence, it can be taken at face value— that is, literally—or even as an ironic negation. Examine the following sentences:

¡**Cualquiera** la hubiera entendido!	*Anybody* would have understood her. *Nobody* would have understood her!
Cualesquiera que sean sus motivos, no me convencerán.	*Whatever* her reasons are, they will not convince me.

EJERCICIO 9·1

Multiple choice. Select the pronoun that best fits the context, and then translate the sentence from Spanish to English.

1. ¡Sal de allí, _____ que seas!
   a. quienquiera
   b. bastante
   c. todo

   _____

2. _____ hay en este archivo que habrá que investigar.
   a. Harto
   b. Ninguno
   c. Mucho

   _____

3. _____ está mal con este programa de computadora.
   a. Demasiado
   b. Algo
   c. Alguien

   _____

4. ¿Hombres valientes? No creo que haya _____ hoy en día.
   a. ninguno
   b. algo
   c. cualquiera

   _____

5. Llamé al número que Ud. me dio pero _____ contestó.
   a. alguno
   b. ninguno
   c. nadie

6. ¿Hay _____ que hable ruso en su compañía?
   a. alguien
   b. nadie
   c. alguno

7. _____ me pareció muy confuso después de que Juan nos lo quiso explicar.
   a. Ninguno
   b. Uno
   c. Todo

8. En esta situación hay _____ que se puede hacer para resolverla. Hay que esperar.
   a. demasiado
   b. poco
   c. todo

9. Si _____ quiere aprender, tendrá que pasar las noches leyendo.
   a. uno
   b. tal
   c. alguno

10. ¿Libros en su casa? ¡Ja! No he visto _____.
    a. uno
    b. ninguno
    c. nada

11. _____ dice ése, pero poco hace.
    a. Mucho
    b. Uno
    c. Algo

    _____

12. _____ hay que dice mentiras sin que le duela la consciencia.
    a. Poco
    b. Tal
    c. Mucho

    _____

13. Busqué por toda la casa tratando de encontrar una guía telefónica pero no

    hallé _____.
    a. alguno
    b. ninguna
    c. poco

    _____

14. _____ lo que hacía en esa época siempre le salía bien.
    a. Todo
    b. Alguno
    c. Quienquiera

    _____

15. No veo _____ en el fondo del lago.
    a. alguien
    b. uno
    c. nada

    _____

16. _____ que sean sus excusas, no las podremos aceptar.
    a. Tal
    b. Nadie
    c. Cualesquiera

    _____

17. No vimos a _____ cuando fuimos a la playa ese día.
    a. nada
    b. nadie
    c. ninguno

    _____

18. Si hay _____ que quieres decirme, debes hacerlo ahora porque me impaciento.
    a. algo
    b. alguien
    c. alguno

    _____

19. ¡_____ lo hubiera hecho así!
    a. Quienesquiera
    b. Cualquiera
    c. Cualquier

    _____

20. Íbamos echando agua del fondo de la canoa, _____ mucha,

    _____ poca.
    a. cuál
    b. nada
    c. algo

    _____

Translate the following sentences from Spanish to English.

1. Quien tal hace, tal paga.

   _____

2. Todo lo que reluce no es de oro.

   _____

3. No hay nada que podamos hacer para arreglar el carro.

_____

4. No vi a nadie en la calle.

_____

5. ¿Impuestos? No queremos ninguno.

_____

6. Tal puede ser, pero no lo creo.

_____

7. ¿Hay alguien aquí que pueda explicar el plan?

_____

8. Uno no se enriquece durmiendo.

_____

9. Nada había hecho para que lo trataran tan mal.

_____

10. Puede hacerlo cualquiera; me da lo mismo.

_____

11. Algo pasa y lo voy a averiguar.

_____

12. ¡Cualquiera le hubiera creído!

_____

13. Nada te espante; nada te turbe.

_____

14. Nadie nos llamó.

_____

15. Bastante dijo para que empezáramos a dudarle.

_____

Translate the following sentences from English to Spanish.

1. Tell whoever is at the door that I will be there in a moment.

   _____

2. There is little I can do to help her.

   _____

3. He ate way too much last night.

   _____

4. Do you (*formal, singular*) need something?

   _____

5. I don't need anything.

   _____

6. Is there someone on the phone?

   _____

7. There is no one on the phone.

   _____

8. Magazines? I don't see any.

   _____

9. Newspapers? I see some.

   _____

10. He has plenty of money to buy the car.

    _____

11. He does too much.

    _____

12. Much is said but little is done to help the poor.

    _____

13. Find whomever you (*formal, singular*) can, so long as he speaks Chinese.

_____

14. She didn't meet anyone interesting at the party.

_____

15. There is something she needs to tell you (*formal, singular*).

_____

Answer key

1 Subject pronouns

1·1
1. she
2. she
3. he
4. he
5. we
6. I
7. you
8. they
9. we
10. you
11. you
12. you
13. you
14. you
15. he

1·2
1. él
2. tú
3. nosotros; nosotras *(if the speaker is female)*
4. yo
5. ustedes
6. vosotros *(Spain)*; ustedes *(Latin America)*
7. ellas
8. ellos
9. ellos
10. vosotros *(Spain)*; ustedes *(Latin America)*
11. nosotros *(all males or mixed group)*; nosotras *(speaker and all in group are female)*
12. usted
13. vosotras *(Spain)*; ustedes *(Latin America)*
14. ustedes
15. nosotros *(speaker and all coworkers are male or mixed group)*; nosotras *(if speaker and all coworkers are female)*
16. ellos
17. ellos
18. él
19. ellos

20. ella
21. tú
22. él
23. tú
24. él
25. ella

1·3

1. Sí, él.
2. Sí, usted.
3. Sí, ellas.
4. Sí, tú.
5. Sí, ellos.
6. Sí, ella.
7. Sí, él.
8. Sí, ellos.
9. Sí, él.
10. Sí, ellos.
11. Sí, ella.
12. Sí, ellos.
13. Sí, él.
14. Sí, ellos.
15. Sí, él.
16. Sí, ella.
17. Sí, ellas.
18. Sí, él.
19. Sí, vosotros (*Spain*); ustedes (*Latin America*)
20. Sí, nosotros.

1·4

1. Tú hablas español.
2. Yo veo la película.
3. Ellos corren mucho.
4. Él tiene una hermana.
5. Mi amigo va a Honduras. *Remember that the third person singular verb form is used when speaking of* **él** (*he*) *and* **ella** (*she*) *or when directly addressing a person formally, that is, when speaking to someone whom you address as* **usted** (*the formal, or polite form*).
6. Ellas leen el periódico.
7. La mamá de Enrique trabaja en la ciudad.
8. Yo viajo a España este verano.
9. Usted come el desayuno en la cafetería.
10. Ustedes viven en Guadalajara. *Remember that the third person plural verb form is used when speaking of* **ellos** (*they, either masculine only or inclusive of both genders*) *and* **ellas** (*they, exclusively feminine*) *or when directly addressing any group of people formally or informally (in Latin America), or (in Spain) when speaking to people whom you must address as* **ustedes** (*the formal, or polite form*) *as opposed to* **vosotros** (*the familiar plural form*).
11. Yo pago con tarjetas de crédito.
12. Mi hija prefiere jugar en el jardín.
13. Mi hermana y Juana necesitan estudiar más.
14. Nosotros compramos comida en el mercado.

15. Vosotros escribís cartas todos los días.
16. Ellos venden motocicletas.
17. Mi papá le da flores a nuestra mamá.
18. Tú nos visitas los fines de semana.
19. Su hermano piensa mucho en las películas.
20. Mis hijos duermen ocho horas cada noche.

1·5
1. ¿Ella mira?
2. ¿Él va?
3. ¿Yo estudio?
4. ¿Enrique y María viajan? *Remember that* **él** *plus* **ella** *equals* **ellos**—*just as* he *plus* she *logically equals* they.
5. ¿Ellas ven?
6. ¿Nosotros dormimos?
7. ¿Tú lees?
8. ¿Tú y yo escribimos? *Remember that* **tú** *plus* **yo** *equals* **nosotros**—*just as* you *plus* I *logically equals* we.
9. ¿Nosotros necesitamos?
10. ¿Juan busca?
11. ¿Ellos ponen?
12. ¿Usted vuelve?
13. ¿Yo tengo?
14. ¿Yo estoy?
15. ¿Ustedes dicen?
16. ¿Tú sales?
17. ¿La Sra. Martínez paga?
18. ¿Mis tíos salen?
19. ¿Yo soy?
20. ¿Vosotros trabajáis?

1·6
1. compro
2. va
3. puedes
4. acompaño
5. ponen
6. vamos
7. cambio
8. escuchan
9. pido
10. trabajamos
11. sirven
12. debes
13. salgo
14. pensamos
15. canta
16. vuelven

17. vas *Note that the subject pronoun* **tú** *appears at the end of the sentence. Spanish word order is more flexible than English, partly because certain forms have only one function;* **tú** *cannot be anything but a subject pronoun.*
18. pongo
19. sé
20. sigue

2 Reflexive object pronouns

2·1 *When conjugating reflexive verbs, there are two common errors. One is forgetting to make the reflexive pronoun (in its infinitive and third person forms,* **se**) *agree with the subject. Another common error is forgetting to place the pronoun in front of the verb (when no helping verb is involved and therefore no other position is possible).*

1. Yo me levanto.   *I get up.*
2. Ella se acuesta.   *She goes to bed.*
3. Yo me pongo.   *I put on.*
4. Vosotros os dormís.   *You fall asleep.*
5. Él se cansa.   *He gets tired.*
6. Ella se ve.   *She sees herself.*
7. Nosotros nos despertamos.   *We wake up.*
8. Yo me enfado.   *I get mad.*
9. Tú te secas.   *You dry yourself.*
10. Tú te preocupas.   *You worry.*
11. Usted se entristece.   *You get sad.*
12. Ellas se maquillan.   *They put on makeup.*
13. Ustedes se alegran.   *You (plural) get happy.*
14. Ellos se deprimen.   *They get depressed.*
15. Nosotros nos lavamos.   *We wash ourselves (or each other).*
16. Yo me río.   *I laugh.*
17. Él se enferma.   *He gets sick.*
18. Ustedes se duchan.   *You (plural) (take a) shower.*
19. Ellas se mojan.   *They get wet.*
20. Vosotros os cepilláis.   *You brush your (or each others') hair.*

2·2
1. b
2. c
3. c
4. a
5. b
6. b
7. c
8. a
9. b
10. b
11. c
12. b
13. a

14. b
15. b
16. b
17. a
18. b
19. a
20. a

2·3
1. Juan se duerme.
2. Teresa y María se despiertan.
3. Tú y yo nos levantamos./Ud. y yo nos levantamos.
4. Mis amigos se caen.
5. Usted se enoja.
6. Los niños se abrazan.
7. Mi mamá se alegra.
8. Tomás y José se enferman.
9. Sus amigos se ríen.
10. Él y yo nos preocupamos.
11. Nosotros nos cansamos.
12. Ella se deprime.
13. Tomás y José se mejoran.
14. Ellas se maquillan.
15. Yo me enfermo.
16. Ella se entristece.
17. Ella y yo nos besamos.
18. Ellos se ven.
19. Ellos se duchan.
20. Nos lavamos las manos.

3 Direct object pronouns

3·1
1. c
2. f
3. d
4. e
5. b
6. g
7. c
8. a
9. g
10. f

3·2
1. me
2. la
3. nos
4. las
5. la
6. lo

7. te
8. lo (el pastel); la (la tarta)
9. lo
10. lo
11. las
12. os
13. la
14. lo (*if male*); la (*if female*)
15. los
16. lo/la *Remember that* **usted** *takes on the gender of the person whom one is addressing.*
17. nos
18. los
19. nos
20. lo

3·3
1. B
2. E
3. B
4. E
5. E
6. B
7. E
8. B
9. B
10. E
11. E
12. E
13. B
14. B
15. E
16. B
17. B
18. E
19. E
20. E

3·4
1. a. Nosotros llevamos la comida.
   b. comida
   c. la
   d. Nosotros la llevamos.
2. a. Ella ve a María.
   b. María
   c. la
   d. Ella la ve.
3. a. Ellos deben contar la historia.
   b. historia
   c. la
   d. Ellos la deben contar./Ellos deben contarla.

4. a. Tú lees los libros.
   b. libros
   c. los
   d. Tú los lees.
5. a. Él escribe una carta.
   b. carta
   c. la
   d. Él la escribe.
6. a. Ustedes envían los regalos.
   b. regalos
   c. los
   d. Ustedes los envían.
7. a. Ella va a comprar un abrigo.
   b. abrigo
   c. lo
   d. Ella lo va a comprar./Ella va a comprarlo.
8. a. Ellos desean vender la casa.
   b. casa
   c. la
   d. Ellos la desean vender./Ellos desean venderla.
9. a. Nosotros hacemos el pan.
   b. pan
   c. lo
   d. Nosotros lo hacemos.
10. a. Usted alquila un apartamento.
    b. apartamento
    c. lo
    d. Usted lo alquila.
11. a. Ellos reducen la contaminación.
    b. contaminación
    c. la
    d. Ellos la reducen.
12. a. Él dirige la orquesta.
    b. orquesta
    c. la
    d. Él la dirige.
13. a. Ella quiere a sus hijos.
    b. hijos
    c. los
    d. Ella los quiere.
14. a. Ellos preparan las comidas.
    b. comidas
    c. las
    d. Ellos las preparan.
15. a. Él va a dejar los dulces en la mesa.
    b. dulces
    c. los
    d. Él los va a dejar en la mesa./Él va a dejarlos en la mesa.

16. a. Nosotros vamos a contar las camisas.
    b. camisas
    c. las
    d. Nosotros las vamos a contar./Nosotros vamos a contarlas.
17. a. Él está poniendo el libro en la mesa.
    b. libro
    c. lo
    d. Él lo está poniendo en la mesa./Él está poniéndolo en la mesa.
18. a. Yo uso vino para cocinar.
    b. vino
    c. lo
    d. Yo lo uso para cocinar.
19. a. Ella puede resolver el problema.
    b. problema
    c. lo
    d. Ella lo puede resolver./Ella puede resolverlo.
20. a. Yo necesito cubrir la motocicleta porque va a llover.
    b. motocicleta
    c. la
    d. Yo la necesito cubrir porque va a llover./Yo necesito cubrirla porque va a llover.

3·5 *Object pronouns are placed after, and attached to, affirmative commands, and between the **no** and the command, for the negative ones.*

1. ¡No lo vendas!
2. ¡Tráelas!
3. ¡No los rompamos!
4. ¡Límpielas!
5. ¡Míralo!
6. ¡No las mires!
7. ¡Escríbala!
8. ¡Mándenlos!
9. ¡Vístalos!
10. ¡No los ponga en la mesa!
11. ¡No los distribuya!
12. ¡Arréglela!
13. ¡Ayúdanos!
14. ¡Quítalos del sofá!
15. ¡No me grites!
16. ¡Sáquenlos!
17. ¡Vendámosla!
18. ¡Ábrelas!
19. ¡No la toques!
20. ¡Bórrelo!

3·6
1. ¡Lávalo!
2. ¡Tírela!/¡Láncela!
3. ¡No nos griten!
4. ¡Preparémosla!

5. ¡Mírala!
6. ¡Quémenlas!
7. ¡No la abras!
8. ¡Tráigala!
9. ¡Manéjenlo!
10. ¡No lo preparemos!
11. ¡Búscalo!
12. ¡Límpialo!
13. ¡No los olvide!
14. ¡Págalas!
15. ¡No la lleves!
16. ¡Llévelo!
17. ¡Dila!
18. ¡No la digas!
19. ¡Léanlo!
20. ¡No lo alquile!

4 Indirect object pronouns

4·1
1. c
2. h
3. i
4. k
5. m
6. o
7. f
8. a
9. d
10. e
11. n
12. j
13. b
14. g
15. l

4·2
1. Él se lo da.
2. Ellos me la mandan.
3. Yo te lo envío.
4. Tú se lo quieres entregar./Tú quieres entregárselo.
5. Ella se la va a regalar./Ella va a regalársela.
6. Nosotros no se lo queremos prestar./Nosotros no queremos prestárselo.
7. Yo no se lo voy a transmitir./Yo no voy a transmitírselo.
8. Los jefes se las proveen.
9. La compañía no se lo suministra.
10. El presidente se lo va a conferir./El presidente va a conferírselo.
11. Los vendedores se los distribuyen.
12. El político se lo dirige.

13. Yo no se la pago.
14. Ella no me la dice.
15. El maestro se la tiene que repetir./El maestro tiene que repetírsela.
16. Los niños se las escriben.
17. El reportero nos la va a comunicar./El reportero va a comunicárnosla.
18. El astrónomo se la indica.
19. La asistente de vuelo se la dice.
20. Mis padres se lo dan.

4·3
1. ¡Cuénteselo!
2. ¡No se lo cuentes!
3. ¡Indíquensela!
4. ¡Enseñádselas!
5. ¡Díctasela!
6. ¡Muéstremelo!
7. ¡Véndanselas!
8. ¡No se las digas!
9. ¡Entregádsela!
10. ¡Confiéraselo!
11. ¡Envíaselo!
12. ¡Préstenselo!
13. ¡No se las presten!
14. ¡Transmítanosla!
15. ¡Repítesela!
16. ¡No me los escribas!
17. ¡No se lo provea!
18. ¡No se la dirijan!
19. ¡Regálaselo!
20. ¡No se la paguéis!

4·4
1. John gives them to me.
2. I say it to them.
3. She always tells me it.
4. He/she sends them to us by airmail.
5. We're going to sell it to you.
6. They are going to send them to you.
7. We are reading it to the children.
8. You are going to buy them for me.
9. Teach it to him/her/them! *or* Show it to him/her/them!
10. I am going to distribute them to my customers.
11. They are going to write it to/for us.
12. John repeats it to the students.
13. You show it to him/her/them on the map.
14. Don't tell it to him/her/them!
15. I give it to them.
16. Loan it to me!
17. They turn it in to you every week.
18. You want to comment on it to us.

19. The bosses communicate it to me each morning.
20. He does not want to tell it to me.

4·5
1. Vamos a mostrárselos./Se los vamos a mostrar.
2. Ellos quieren traérnoslos./Ellos nos los quieren traer.
3. Ella va a mandársela./Ella se la va a mandar. *(or* enviársela/enviar*)*
4. ¿Deseas hacérnoslo?/¿Nos lo deseas hacer?
5. ¡Cómpramelo!
6. Ellos no van a dictárnoslo./Ellos no nos lo van a dictar.
7. Yo se las envío.
8. Ella me la dice.
9. ¿Va a prestárselo Ud.?/¿Se lo va a prestar Ud.?
10. Ella va a escribírsela./Ella se la va a escribir.
11. Él está comprándoselo./Él se lo está comprando.
12. Los niños están distribuyéndolos./Los niños los están distribuyendo.
13. ¿Van a entregárselo hoy Uds.?/¿Se lo van a entregar Uds. hoy?
14. El maestro no quiere tener que repetírsela./El maestro no se la quiere tener que repetir.
15. ¡Véndaselo!
16. ¡Repítemelo! *(or, if* **historia** *is the direct object noun,* ¡Repítemela!*)*
17. ¡Dígansela!
18. Ellos están suministrándonoslas./Ellos nos las están suministrando.
19. Voy a pagárselo mañana./Se lo voy a pagar mañana.
20. Ella desea revelárselos esta noche./Ella se los desea revelar esta noche.

5 The uses of se

5·1
1. D I sell them to my colleagues.
2. I In Colombia, a lot of coffee is produced.
3. E When I heard the noise, I left the restaurant right away *(i.e., I "split")*.
4. P The sofa got ruined. *("It ruined itself" is absurd.)*
5. R My brother fell asleep early.
6. I They drink coffee and tea in Seattle.
7. R The tourists ran out of money. *(Literally, The tourists' money ran out on them.)*
8. R We are running out of time. *(Literally, Time is running out on us.)*
9. I They were looking for Emilio Escobar. *("Se busca" is used on wanted posters.)*
10. E We ran out of food on account of the kids' appetites. *(Literally, The food gave out on us because of the kids' appetites.)*
11. D They gave it to them.
12. R The general surrendered after the battle. *(Literally, The general gave himself up after the battle.)*
13. I They show French and Spanish films in that theater.
14. I From the lookout, one can see the whole city.
15. E The cows devoured the corn.

5·2
1. Does your money run out at the end of the month?
2. They are going to give them to him/her/them/you *(formal)* tomorrow.
3. Poor Mary, her son died.
4. They serve a lot of interesting dishes on that street.

5. We already gave the shirts to my mother.
6. My tire went flat.
7. John's lights went out on him during the storm.
8. That John—he didn't want to listen to us and he went away grumbling.
9. Those medieval ideas went to his head and he became a knight errant.
10. Suddenly, a solution to the problem came to me.
11. In Cuba they dance to the tunes of rural music.
12. I know people look for boyfriends and girlfriends online.
13. She bowed her head when they accused her of the crime.
14. My computer freezes up on me a lot.
15. The teenagers ate up all the spaghetti.
16. When the alarm goes off, he gets up.
17. The rabbit scurried away from the hunters through the bushes.
18. When one is a student, one reads a lot and eats little.
19. The money? John already gave it to Thomas.
20. The device got damaged.

5·3
1. El ladrón se fue corriendo.
2. Se busca a Jesse James.
3. Se le fue el esposo a Katalina.
4. Los obreros se durmieron.
5. Se vende auto.
6. Se le perdió la bolsa.
7. Los niños se subieron el árbol.
8. Ellos se comieron la pizza.
9. Se nos escapó el tiempo.
10. Se encuentra buena comida en Acapulco.
11. Se trancó la puerta.
12. Se le cayó el árbol encima.
13. Se les vino la idea.
14. Se le murió el gato.
15. Se abre a la nueve y se cierra a las cinco.
16. Cuando se es pobre, se tiene que trabajar más.
17. Se alquilan apartamentos.
18. Se contesta el teléfono cuando suena.
19. Se le arruinó el vestido.
20. Se hablan español y francés aquí.

6 Pronouns as objects of prepositions

6·1
1. mí
2. -tigo
3. Ud.
4. tú, yo
5. él
6. ti
7. ellos

8. ella
9. él
10. -sigo
11. tú
12. yo
13. yo
14. ti
15. él
16. ti
17. -sigo
18. tú
19. ella
20. -migo

6·2
1. We do not want to speak with him.
2. According to them, there is no global warming.
3. In front of her, a skyscraper can be seen.
4. John has hidden it behind himself.
5. Do they want to go to the beach with you?
6. Between him and her, there is always peace and harmony.
7. I prefer the shirt that is behind you.
8. She is going to discuss it with you.
9. I believe this gift is for you.
10. In front of them, she declared her love to him.
11. Behind you, there is an important monument.
12. Theresa is taking it with her.
13. There are no arguments among/between them.
14. The criminal appears before him.
15. If you leave, they'll follow after you.
16. Jane and Thomas are taking it with them.
17. The contrary opinion is yours, not mine.
18. She wants to scale the mountain with you.
19. Because of me, the cake got ruined.
20. John is sick, so we are going to do it in his place.

6·3
1. Ellos desean ir contigo.
2. Ella está detrás de él.
3. Estoy en contra de ellos.
4. Ella se habla a sí misma./Ella habla consigo misma.
5. Ellos están delante de Uds.
6. ¿Va a venir ella con Ud.?
7. Según él, no hay ningún problema.
8. Por/Debido a ti, estoy contento/a.
9. Por ti, daría el mundo.
10. Sin ella, Juan está triste.
11. Ellos salen del edificio, detrás de ellos.
12. ¿Vas a ir al cine conmigo?
13. No hay nadie para mí excepto ella.

14. Él está resolviendo el problema sin nosotros.
15. Quiero vivir la vida junto a ti.
16. Ella quiere vivir la vida junto a mí.
17. No sé cómo ella puede vivir sin mí.
18. El jefe tiene cincuenta personas debajo de él.
19. Ellos no hablan de Ud.
20. Además de ti, vienen cinco personas mañana.

7 Demonstrative, possessive, and interrogative pronouns

7·1 *Remember that there are three relative distances involved when dealing with demonstrative adjectives, which extend to their pronominal forms.*

1. l
2. k
3. g
4. d
5. j
6. a
7. b
8. e
9. f
10. i
11. c
12. h

7·2 *Remember that the gender and number of possessive pronouns follow the gender and number of the thing possessed, not the gender or number of the possessor.*

1. g
2. a
3. k
4. j
5. f
6. b
7. c
8. i
9. d
10. h
11. l
12. e

7·3
1. aquélla (*A demonstrative pronoun, referring to* **una tienda** *distant from the speakers.*)
2. mías (*A possessive pronoun, referring to* **amigas** *the speaker shares with Theresa.*)
3. ésta (*A demonstrative pronoun, referring to* **una blusa** *close to the speaker.*)
4. ésa (*A demonstrative pronoun, referring to another* **blusa** *near both speakers, but not as near as the first.*)

5. aquélla (*A demonstrative pronoun, referring to a third* **blusa**, *farthest away from both speakers.*)
6. quién (*An interrogative pronoun, asking whom the present is for.*)
7. Esa (*A demonstrative adjective, modifying* **muchacha**, *psychologically equidistant from both speakers because she is not physically present.*)
8. Ésa (*The pronominal form of the previous demonstrative adjective, referring to the same young woman.*)
9. cuál (*An interrogative pronoun seeking to elicit a choice between two different* **blusas**.)
10. ésta (*A demonstrative pronoun, referring to a* **blusa rosada** *being held up by the speaker for inspection, along with the* **blusa azul**.)
11. ésta (*A demonstrative pronoun referring to the* **blusa azul**, *close to both speakers.*)
12. suyo (*A third person possessive pronoun referring to* **el color** *that is best for Elena, that is "her" color.*)
13. míos (*A possessive pronoun referring to* **los ojos** *of the speaker.*)
14. Aquél (*A demonstrative pronoun referring to* **un hotel** *distant from both speakers.*)
15. Qué (*An interrogative pronoun asking* what *type of hotel Las Brisas is.*)

8 Relative pronouns

8·1 *Remember that* **que** *or* **quien(es)** *can be used to refer to people, but that* **quien(es)** *must be used if the relative pronoun is preceded by a preposition. Thus, since no preposition precedes the relative pronouns in numbers 10, 14, or 15, either* **que** *or* **quien(es)** *is admissible.*

1. quien
2. que
3. que
4. quienes
5. que
6. quienes
7. quienes
8. que
9. quienes
10. que/quienes
11. que
12. quienes
13. que
14. que/quien
15. que/quienes

8·2 *If this exercise is difficult, redo it, first identifying the antecedents and noting their gender and number. Then it should be quite simple.*

1. el cual
2. los cuales
3. las cuales
4. los cuales
5. los cuales
6. las cuales
7. los cuales

8. el cual
9. lo cual
10. lo cual
11. la cual
12. los cuales
13. los cuales
14. lo cual
15. la cual

8·3
1. I see the sun that shines on us with its rays.
2. When I heard what she had done, I got mad.
3. I have several records from the 50s, which seem comical to me now.
4. The horses stampeded from the corral, while the cowboys, who should have chased after them, seemed not to know what to do.
5. The train that left early had a mechanical problem two hours later.
6. There were a lot of trees in the garden of Mr. Salazar, who decided to leave only three.
7. There were so many trees in Mr. Salazar's garden that he decided to cut them down.
8. There are so many politicians who lie to us so much that you/one can't believe them.
9. The authors of the novels about whom the poet spoke to me died very young.
10. On account of tuberculosis, the novelists who wrote in the nineteenth century usually did not live very long.

8·4
1. Pronto veremos a nuestra tía que/quien vive en Seattle.
2. La casa es muy bonita, para aquéllos a quienes les gusta ese estilo.
3. Hay muchas cosas en el mundo que requieren nuestra atención.
4. ¿Es éste el libro de que/del cual te hablé?
5. ¿Es ése el tipo con quien saliste la semana pasada?
6. Éstos son los niños para quienes compramos regalos.
7. Ésta es el arma con que/la cual disparó al oso.
8. Las plumas en la mesa, que/las cuales son costosas, eran regalos.
9. ¿Es ella la muchacha que/quien te llamó?
10. Al rey le gusta jugar, lo cual es bueno.

9 Indefinite pronouns

9·1
1. a Get out of here, **whoever** you are!
2. c There is **much** in this file that will have to be investigated.
3. b **Something** is wrong with this computer program.
4. a Brave men? I don't think there are **any** nowadays. *(The double negative is required in Spanish.)*
5. c I called the number you gave me but **no one** answered.
6. a Is there **someone** who speaks Russian in your company?
7. c **Everything** seemed very confusing after John tried to explain it to us.
8. b In this situation, there is **little** that can be done to resolve it. We'll have to wait.
9. a If **one** wishes to learn, he'll have to spend the nights reading.
10. b Books in his house? Ha! I haven't seen a single one. *(The double negative is required in Spanish.)*

11. a That fellow talks **much** but does little.
12. b There are **such people** who tell lies without it hurting their conscience. *(Note that the singular **tal** in Spanish refers to a class of people in this proverbial usage.)*
13. b I searched the whole house for a phone book but could not find **one**. *(The double negative is required in Spanish.)*
14. a **Everything** he used to do back then would turn out well.
15. c I don't see **anything** at the bottom of the lake. *(The double negative is required in Spanish.)*
16. c Whatever her excuses may be, we will not be able to accept them.
17. b We didn't see **anyone** when we went to the beach that day. *(In addition to the need for the double negative, note the use of the* personal **a** *before the blank, making **nadie** the only possible answer.)*
18. a If there is **something** you wish to say to me, you should say it now, because I am losing my patience.
19. b **Anybody** would have done it that way!
20. a We were bailing water from the bottom of the canoe, **some of us** a lot, **some of us** a little.

9·2
1. Whoso thus doeth, thus payeth.
2. All that glitters is not gold.
3. There is nothing we can do to fix the car.
4. I saw no one in the street.
5. Taxes? We do not want any.
6. It could be thus, but I do not believe it.
7. Is there someone here who can explain the plan?
8. One does not grow rich by sleeping.
9. He had not done anything to make them treat him so badly.
10. Anyone can do it; it does not matter to me.
11. Something is going on and I am going to find it out.
12. Anyone might have believed him/her! *(Or ironically: Nobody would have believed him/her!)*
13. Let nothing frighten you; let nothing disturb you.
14. No one called us.
15. He said enough to make us begin to doubt him.

9·3
1. Dile a quienquiera que esté en la puerta que vengo enseguida.
2. Hay poco que puedo hacer para ayudarla.
3. Se comió harta comida anoche.
4. ¿Necesita Ud. algo?
5. No necesito nada.
6. ¿Hay alguien en el teléfono?
7. No hay nadie en el teléfono.
8. ¿Revistas? No veo ninguna.
9. ¿Periódicos? Veo algunos.
10. Él tiene suficiente dinero para comprarse el auto.
11. Él hace demasiado.
12. Mucho se dice pero poco se hace para ayudar a los pobres.
13. Busque a quien pueda, mientras que hable chino.
14. Ella no conoció a nadie que fuera interesante en la fiesta.
15. Hay algo que ella tiene que decirle a Ud.